THE TERRORISM TRAP

Additional Books by Michael Parenti

To Kill a Nation: The Attack on Yugoslavia (2000)

History as Mystery (1999)

America Besieged (1998)

Blackshirts and Reds (1997)

Dirty Truths (1996)

Against Empire (1995)

Democracy for the Few (7th edition 2001)

Land of Idols: Political Mythology in America (1994)

Inventing Reality: The Politics of News Media (1986, 1993)

Make-Believe Media: The Politics of Entertainment (1992)

The Sword and the Dollar (1989)

Power and the Powerless (1978)

Ethnic and Political Attitudes (1975)

Trends and Tragedies in American Foreign Policy (1971)

The Anti-Communist Impulse (1969)

THE
TERRORISM TRAP

SEPTEMBER 11 AND BEYOND

MICHAEL PARENTI

CITY LIGHTS BOOKS
San Francisco

Cover design by Stefan Gutermuth
Cover photo by June Felter
Book design by Nancy J. Peters
Typography by Harvest Graphics

Library of Congress Cataloging-in-Publication Data

Parenti, Michael, 1933–
    The terrorism trap : September 11 and beyond / Michael
    Parenti.
    p.   cm.
    Includes bibliographical references.
    ISBN 0-87286-405-7
    1. United States — Foreign relations — 1989–
2. United States — Politics and government — 1989–
3. United States — Military policy.   4. Intervention
(International law)   5. September 11 Terrorist Attacks, 2001.
6. War on Terrorism, 2001–   7. Militarism — Political
aspects — United States.   8. Militarism — Economic aspects
— United States.   9. Corporations — Social aspects —
United States.   10. Globalization — Social aspects.
I. Title.
E840'.P268 2001
973.931—dc21   2002017426

CITY LIGHTS BOOKS are edited by Lawrence Ferlinghetti and
Nancy J. Peters and published at the City Lights Bookstore,
261 Columbus Avenue, San Francisco, CA 94133.
www.citylights.com

ACKNOWLEDGMENTS

An expression of gratitude to the following: Nancy J. Peters of City Lights Books who spurred me on to write this book with the promise of swift publication, and who gave it an essential final read; Marilyn Bechtel who lent her expertise to the chapter on Afghanistan; and Jane Scantlebury who provided an abundance of useful materials, helpful ideas, and a cogent critique of the entire manuscript. Peggy Karp, formerly Peggy Noton, has assisted me on various writing projects in the past, and to her the book is dedicated.

To Peggy Karp

TABLE OF CONTENTS

1   TERRORISM MEETS REACTIONISM

ON THE MORNING OF SEPTEMBER 11, 2001, terrorists hijacked four US commercial airliners and managed to plow two of them into the twin towers of New York's World Trade Center and another into the Pentagon, the home offices of the US Department of Defense, for an estimated loss of some 3000 lives. In the immediate aftermath of this horrific tragedy, almost-elected president George W. Bush announced his "war on terrorism." What he left unannounced was his campaign to advance the agenda of the reactionary Right at home and abroad. This included rolling back an already mangled federal human services sector, reverting to deficit spending for the benefit of a wealthy creditor class, increasing the repression of dissent, and expanding to a still greater magnitude the budgets and global reach of the US military and other components of the national security state. Indeed, within days after the terrorist attacks, the *Wall Street Journal* called on Bush to take advantage of the "unique political climate" to "assert his leadership not just on security and foreign policy but across the board." It summoned the president to push quickly for more tax-rate cuts, expanded oil drilling in Alaska, fast-track authority for trade negotiations, and raids on the Social Security surplus.[1] This is exactly what he did.

More for War

Bush himself noted that the September 11 attacks offered "an opportunity" to "strengthen America." As numerous conservatives spoke eagerly of putting the country on a permanent war footing, the president proudly declared "the first war of the twenty-first century" against an unspecified enemy to extend over an indefinite time frame.

Swept along in the jingoist tide, that gaggle of political wimps known as the US Congress passed a War Powers Resolution Authorization, granting Bush the power to initiate military action against any nation, organization, or individual of his choosing, without ever having to proffer evidence to justify the attack. Such an unlimited grant of arbitrary power—in violation of international law, the UN charter, and the US Constitution—transforms the almost-elected president into an absolute monarch who can exercise life-and-death power over any quarter of the world. Needless to say, numerous other nations have greeted the president's elevation to King of the Planet with something less than enthusiasm.

And King of the Planet is how he began to act, bombing an already badly battered and impoverished Afghanistan on the suspicion that Osama bin Laden, who was now situated in that country, masterminded the September 11 attacks. Bush's godlike deliverance of death and destruction upon Afghan civilians was entitled "Operation Infinite Justice." When it was pointed out that Muslims might be offended because of their belief that only Allah can dispense infinite justice, the White House renamed the bombing campaign "Operation Enduring Freedom." Even the normally sycophantic press did not rightly warm up to this promotional labeling.

Unmentioned in all this was the fact that US leaders had actively fostered and financed the rise of the Taliban and bin Laden.[2] By December, flushed with victory against the Taliban, Bush was airily announcing that he might next attack Iraq. Vice-President Dick

Cheney referred ominously to "forty or fifty countries" that could need military disciplining.[3] One of these seemed to be the United States itself, at least if we heed Deputy Defense Secretary Paul Wolfowitz, who urged that US armed forces be allowed to engage in domestic law enforcement, a responsibility that has been denied the military since 1878.

Under pressure to present a united front against terrorism, Democratic legislators rolled over on the issue of military spending. Opposition to the so-called outer-space missile defense shield ("National Missile Defense") began to evaporate, as did willingness to preserve the Anti-Ballistic Missile Treaty (ABM). The lawmakers seemed ready to come up with most of the $8.3 billion that the White House said it needed to develop the missile defense shield and further militarize outer space. In December, Bush declared that the United States was unilaterally breaking the ABM treaty with Russia, saying that it "hinders us from developing an anti-missile shield that will deter an attack from a rogue state."[4]

Congress marched in lockstep behind Bush's proposal to jack up the military budget to $360 billion for 2002. Additional funds were promised to the NSA, CIA, FBI, and other skulduggery units of what has come to be known as the US national security state.[5]

Having been shown that the already gargantuan

defense budget was not enough to stop a group of suicidal hijackers armed with box cutters, Bush and Congress thought it best to pour still more money into the pockets of the military-industrial cartel. Incidentally, the United States spends more on arms than all the other major industrial nations combined. The US military budget is about seven times greater than the $51 billion spent by Russia, the next highest competitor.

Wag the Dog

Many of the measures taken to "fight terrorism" have little to do with actual security and are public relations ploys designed to (a) heighten the nation's siege psychology and (b) demonstrate that the government has things under control. Hours after the September 11 attacks, the US Navy deployed aircraft carriers off the coast of New York to "guard the city," as if a mass invasion were in the offing. National guardsmen dressed in combat fatigues and armed with automatic weapons patrolled the airports. Flights were canceled until further notice. Sidewalk baggage check-ins and electronic tickets were prohibited for a time, all supposedly to create greater security.

Since increased airport security leads to greater inconvenience, it was decided that greater inconvenience would somehow increase security—or at least give that appearance. It did not fool many people. In my post-September 11 sojourns, I spoke to a number of passengers who agreed that air travel had become more inconvenient but not really more secure. Indeed, 95 percent of the checked baggage still was going through without being x-rayed. And the underpaid employees who peered into the dim little screens at the security gate could be fooled as easily as ever. "Many screeners have to work two or more jobs, leaving them tired and distracted as they scan thousands of objects per hour for tiny but potentially significant signs of danger," noted a report by the Service Employees International Union.[6] An acquaintance of mine informed me that his Swiss Army knife, which he unknowingly had in his carry-on bag, passed scrutiny with no challenge both on his departing and return flights in November 2001.

Hopefully, things will improve. Checked baggage and carry-ons reportedly will be subjected to more sophisticated electronic scanning. But right now one can only marvel at how little real internal security has been put into place, not just at airports but at water reservoirs, chemical factories, nuclear plants, bridges, and tunnels.

The biggest public relations ploy of all was the bombing of hillsides and villages in Afghanistan. It left us with the reassuring image of Uncle Sam striking back at the terrorists. Over the last two years the Taliban repeatedly offered to hand over bin Laden, if only the United States would present evidence of his culpability. Subjected to US bombings of their villages and cities, the Taliban then offered to give bin Laden to a third country to stand trial—this time without seeing any evidence against him. Even this major concession was rejected by the White House. It appeared that the primary US goal was displaying US retaliatory power and establishing a military presence in Afghanistan, not apprehending bin Laden and bringing him to justice in a public trial.[7]

Lost in all this is the fact that US leaders have been the greatest purveyors of terrorism throughout the world. In past decades they or their surrogate mercenary forces have unleashed terror bombing campaigns against unarmed civilian populations, destroying houses, schools, hospitals, churches, hotels, factories, farms, bridges, and other nonmilitary targets in scores of countries, causing death and destruction to millions of innocents. Using death squad terrorism US leaders have also been successful in destroying reformist and democratic movements in a number of other countries (discussed in more detail in chapter five). Of course hardly a word of this is uttered in the corporate media, leaving Bush and company free to parade themselves as champions of peace and freedom.

Reactionism on the Home Front

Well before any public officeholder dared to broach the subject, media flacks were proclaiming a need to rollback our liberties. Hardly an hour after the attacks on the World Trade Center, I heard NBC anchorman Tom Brokaw intone, "This is a war zone. This is *war*." The next morning at 8 a.m., less than twenty-four hours after the attacks, another NBC announcer stated, "Some of the freedoms we have we may no longer be able to take for granted and may have to give up." That same morning, ABC produced an instant poll claiming to show that 66 percent of Americans were prepared to "give up some of their civil liberties for a more secure society." Some weeks later, the editor of *New Republic* angered by the public protests against the US bombing of Afghanistan wrote: "This nation is now at war. And in such an environment, domestic political dissent is immoral without a prior statement of national solidairty, a choosing of sides." Meanwhile, Tom Brokaw was at it again, impatiently asking why US ground troops had not been deployed in Afghanistan "in division-size force." And a pundit on Fox News was demanding that US forces invade and occupy Libya and Iraq.[8]

We should realize that the press is not just a stenographer for power, faithfully echoing what authorities feed it. It plays a far more proactive role as propagandist for the ruling ideology, exercising its own initiative to soften up public opinion, telling people what to think about events even before the events have played out, clearing the way for policymakers to make their moves.

Just six weeks after the attacks, Congress overwhelmingly passed the USA PATRIOT Act[9] which places our First Amendment rights to free speech and political association in jeopardy by creating a definition of "domestic terrorism" that includes acts that "appear to be intended to influence the policy of a government by intimidation or coercion." Couched in such broad and vague terms, the act runs the risk of being used against anti-globalization activists and other political dissenters, who can be targeted selectively based on their militant and confrontational opposition to government policies. The act also grants the executive branch unchecked surveillance tools, including an expanded opportunity to track email and Internet usage, conduct roving wiretaps, monitor financial transactions, and obtain educational and medical records. The act strips immigrants of just about all Constitutional protections. In the last four months of 2001, some twelve hundred people were rounded up and put into "preventive detention," with no charges brought against them and no legal redress available to them.[10]

The act invests the Feds with authority to seize all the assets of any organization and its members or any individual deemed to be aiding or abetting "terrorist activity." And it can be applied retroactively without a statute of limitations. Under the new law, a telephone interview I did with Radio Iran in mid-October 2001, trying to explain why US foreign policy is so justifiably hated around the world might qualify me for detention as someone who is abetting terrorism.

The USA PATRIOT Act also allows the CIA to spy openly on Americans. The agency is to share in the collection of a vast array of information from school records, financial transactions, and the Internet, without benefit of court order. The director of the CIA is granted enormous power to gather and disseminate intelligence information drawn from within the United States. This new authority wipes out previous guidelines that protected citizens from unwarranted CIA surveillance.

While all this was going on, Bush issued an executive order allowing the government to bring foreign residents before military tribunals. These trials will be shrouded in secrecy, have a burden of proof that is markedly lower than in any established court of law, and allow for no appeal to a civilian court. It reminded me of a comment ascribed to Groucho Marx: "Military justice is to justice what military music is to music." In keeping with the reactionary Right's agenda, the war against terrorism swiftly became a cover for the war against democratic dissent and public sector services. The message was clear, America must emulate not Athens but Sparta.

One of the White House's earliest efforts at protecting the country from terrorist violence was to cut from the proposed federal budget the $1 billion slated to assist children who are victims of domestic abuse or abandonment. Certainly a nation *at war* has no resources to squander on battered kids or other such frills. Instead, Bush came up with an "emergency package" for the airlines, $5 billion in direct cash and $10 billion in loan guarantees, with the promise of billions more. The airlines were beset by fiscal problems well before the September attacks. This bailout had little to do with fighting terrorism. The real story is that once the industry was deregulated, the airlines began over-capitalizing without sufficient regard for earnings, the assumption being that profits would follow after a company squeezed its competitors to the wall by grabbing a larger chunk of the market. So the profligate diseconomies of unregulated "free market" corporate competition are once more picked up by the US taxpayer—this time in the name of fighting terrorism.

Meanwhile some 80,000 airline employees were laid off in the weeks after September 11, including ticket agents, flight attendants, pilots, mechanics, and ramp workers. They saw not a penny of the windfall reaped by the airline plutocrats and shareholders, whose patriotism did not extend to giving their employees a helping hand.[11] At one point in the House debate, a frustrated Rep. Jay Inslee (D-Wash.) shouted out, "Why in this chamber do the big dogs always eat first?" Inslee was expressing his concerns about the 20,000 to 30,000 Boeing workers who were being let go without any emergency allocation for their families. Sen. Peter G. Fitzgerald (R-Ill.) expressed a similar sentiment when casting the lone dissenting vote in the Senate against the airline bailout: "Congress should be wary of indiscriminately dishing out taxpayer dollars to prop up a failing industry without demanding something in return for taxpayers."

For a time, the post-September 11 anti-terrorism hype served as an excuse to mute opposition to drilling in the Arctic National Wildlife Refuge. Our nation needs oil to maintain its strength and security, we heard. By some estimates, the amount of oil to be extracted from the Arctic preserve would be consumed in the US market within only eight or nine months. It is difficult to see how such drilling would enhance "America's energy self-sufficiency" in the long run, but it would certainly enhance short-term profits for the oil companies. Only a substantial effort to develop solar, tidal, and wind energies can make the country more self-sufficient. These alternative sources are readily available, infinitely renewable, ecologically sound, but—and here's the rub—vastly cheaper and less profitable than oil. Indeed, if developed to any great extent, alternative sustainable energy sources could destroy the multi-billion dollar oil industry, which is why they remain relatively underdeveloped.

Looting the Surplus

The bailout to the airline industry is only part of the spending spree that the White House embarked upon. Bush also endorsed a "stimulus package" of $60 billion to $75 billion to lift the country out of recession by "recharging business investment." He also has called for an additional $60 billion tax cut which, like previous tax reductions, would give meager portions to ordinary folks and lavish sums to fat cats and plutocrats.[12] Where is all this money for defense, war, internal security, airlines, tax cuts, and recharging the economy coming from? Much of it is from the Social Security surplus fund—which is why Bush is so eager to spend, spend, spend.

It is a myth that conservatives are practitioners of fiscal responsibility. Rightwing politicians who sing hymns to a balanced budget have been among the wildest deficit spenders. In twelve years (1981-1992) the Reagan-Bush administrations increased the national debt from $850 billion to $4.5 *trillion*. By early 2000, the debt had climbed to over $5.7 trillion. The deficit is pumped up by two things: first, successive tax cuts to rich individuals and corporations—so that the government increasingly borrows from the wealthy creditors it should be taxing; and second, titanic military budgets. In twelve years, the Reagan-Bush expenditures on the military came to $3.7 trillion. In eight years, Bill Clinton, a conservative Democrat who pretended to talk like a liberal on some subjects, spent over $2 trillion on the military.

Yearly payments on the national debt amount to about $350 billion, representing a colossal upward redistribution of income from working taxpayers to rich creditors. The last two Clinton budgets were the first to trim away the yearly deficit and produce a surplus. The first Bush budget also promised to produce a surplus, almost all of it from Social Security taxes. As a loyal representative of the big financial interests, George II, like his daddy, prefers the upward redistribution of income that comes with a large deficit. The creditor class, composed mostly of superrich individuals and financial institutions, wants this nation to be in debt to it—the same way it wants every other nation to be in debt to it.

Furthermore, the reactionary opponents of Social Security have long argued that the fund will eventually become insolvent and must therefore be privatized (We must destroy the fund in order to save it.) But with Social Security continuing to produce record surpluses, this argument becomes increasingly implausible. By defunding Social Security, either through privatization or deficit spending or both, Bush achieves a key goal of the reactionary agenda.

The Bible says that not everyone who saith "Lord, Lord" shall enter unto the kingdom of heaven. And so not everyone who mouths the sacred shibboleths of patriotism is really concerned about the well-being of his compatriots. Bush and his coterie are prime purveyors of this hypocritical hype, hailing sacrifice and devotion while stuffing their pockets with yet more plunder from the public purse.

2   THE SEPTEMBER 11 IMPERATIVE

THE COMPELLING POLITICO-ECONOMIC
issues, the central imperatives that afflict our nation
and much of the world, are regularly shut out of public
discourse. No one in the corporate media dares to dwell
on how the undemocratic powers of Corporate
America create injustices for Working America, how
wealth for the few creates poverty for the many. No critical examination is offered concerning the inequities of
the tax system, or why this most prosperous nation suf-
fers such gross inadequacies in human services.
Likewise, the threats to the world's ecology posed by
transnational globalization—and the monopolistic
"free trade" treaties like NAFTA, GATT, and FTAA that

undermine our democratic sovereignty—earn hardly a critical glance.

Ignoring US Global Militarism

Never do official circles or corporate media acknowledge how, for more than a half century, US military forces (or their US-supported surrogates) have repeatedly delivered mass destruction upon unarmed civilian populations in Latin America, Asia, Africa, the Middle East, and—with the 1999 bombings of Yugoslavia—even Europe, pernicious acts of terrorism that go unexamined. No critical discussion is offered regarding who really benefits from such ventures and who is harmed. Nothing is said about how the dominant interests within a small number of industrial countries, led by the US national security state continue to monopolize more and more of the world's resources and markets.

US leaders preside over a military force of planetary magnitude unmatched in human history. Every year US taxpayers give up hundreds of billions of their hard-earned dollars to fund this global military empire, whose necessity has never really been critically debated on a national platform. A global military presence, we are told, supposedly safeguards our democracy and something called "the West," discouraging "rogue states" from launching attacks against us, and allowing us to protect weaker nations from aggression. We are told that "US interests" need to be defended, and humanitarian rescue missions must be pursued. Policymakers and media pundits toss these various assertions around like so many advertising slogans, while ignoring the alternative explanations and analyses offered by progressive critics.

With only 5 percent of the earth's population, the United States expends more military funds than all the other major powers combined. The US military establishment consists of about a half-million troops stationed at over 395 major bases and hundreds of minor installations in thirty-five foreign countries; more than 8,000 strategic nuclear weapons and 22,000 tactical ones; a naval strike force greater in total tonnage and firepower than all the other navies of the world combined, consisting of missile cruisers, nuclear submarines, nuclear aircraft carriers, and destroyers that sail every ocean and make port at every continent.

US bomber squadrons and long-range missiles can reach any target, delivering with impunity enough explosive force to destroy the infrastructures of entire countries—as demonstrated against Iraq in 1990-91 and Yugoslavia in 1999. US rapid deployment forces have a firepower in conventional weaponry vastly superior to any other nation's. US satellites and spy planes scope the entire planet. And today Washington is developing a capacity to conduct war from outer space. Worldwide US arms sales to cooperative capitalist nations rose to $36.9 billion in 2000, up from $34 billion in 1999. In addition to sales, since World War II, the US government has given some $240 billion in military aid to train, equip, and subsidized some 2.3 million troops and internal security forces in more than eighty countries, many of them military autocracies. This extraordinary situation, this global military colossus goes on its grim and fatal way largely unexamined and unquestioned in public life.

Filling the National Void

With all these key issues systematically suppressed—relegated at best to small circulation publications and low visibility groups on the left—a void is created in our national discourse. We have a polity that does not treat the central imperatives of public policy in any meaningful or revealing way, a democracy devoid of the democratic debate that might challenge the ideology and practices of its leadership. The media attempt to fill this void with endless puffery, limited secondary issues, public personality profiles, and various scandal stories.

Then came the September 11 terrorist attack on the World Trade Center and the Pentagon. This horrific event gave opinion makers an issue of compelling centrality, equal to any of the ones they have suppressed, but one that could be selectively treated with *conservative* effect, an issue that indicted a fanatical Islamic sect rather than Corporate America or the US national security state.

So for several months the press was consumed by September 11 and its aftermath. Every panel of pundits, every hosted TV show, newspaper editorial, letter to the editor, syndicated column, guest column, and just about every news story dwelled on the terrorist attacks, offering a seemingly infinite constellation of spin-off stories. One favorite was the interviews with various individuals who would say something like: "I was a peacenik during the Vietnam era but this time I am all for bombing the hell out of those terrorists in Afghanistan."

For several months after the attacks, almost as if one's credibility depended upon it, nothing could be communicated without first referencing September 11. The news media were not the only ones laboring under this preoccupation. The editor of a poetry magazine worried that in the "profoundly changed world" created by September 11 "will we now say that poetry is even more irrelevant?" Predictably, he concluded that poetry was *more* important than ever. In similar spirit, stand-up comedians announced that humor was needed more than ever. Movie reviewers wrote that this or that film was a welcome antidote to the horrific events of September 11. Travel writers reassured us that a good vacation (at a safe nearby location) was all the more a healing experience. A restaurant manager in Berkeley, California, told me that her hot soups, a house specialty, were selling well because they were a "comfort food" for persons seeking solace after the September 11 tragedy.

The atomization and alienation that is the common experience of an urban capitalist mass society seemed to be giving way to a community of patriots. Everyone was pulling together to see their way through this crisis. People who normally felt isolated in this dollar-driven Gesellschaft suddenly experienced (and even enjoyed) the solace of huddling together under siege and interacting in a friendlier way with strangers. So the media were filled with stories of New Yorkers who were helping each other, and people all over the nation who were assisting New Yorkers. Looming above all this, were the firemen, police, and working people whose genuine acts of heroism and sacrifice stood in sharp contrast to the opportunistic political pandering emitting from official circles.

For awhile it seemed like the September 11 imperative would continue indefinitely. Sporting events opened with militaristic patriotic commemorations. All the mail that crossed my desk, including subscription and fund raising appeals from every organization imaginable—from the Yale Alumni Association to the Center for Cuban Studies—felt compelled to reference September 11 before launching into their pitch. Friends wrote or called to say they were "doing as well as might be expected in this post 9/11 world."

What was so world-shattering about the terrorist attacks of that day? Why was that event so much more significant than the thousands of other terrorist attacks that have occurred over the last half century? In a word, it all happened in New York City and Washington, D.C., and a strikingly large number of Americans were killed, some 3100 by latest count. Whatever the final toll, it remains the largest single act of terrorism on US soil in the history of this country.

To repeat, the September 11 victims were almost all *Americans* not Iraqis, Yugoslavs, Panamanians, Haitians, Salvadorans, Guatemalans, Vietnamese, Laotians, Angolans, and Mozambiqans—to mention some of the unarmed civilian populations that have been subjected to US mass terror killings in recent decades. The message was taken to heart: one American life is worth countless non-American lives. The ensuing war repeated the equation: the death of one CIA operative in Afghanistan, Mike Spann, was given fulsome treatment in the media while the deaths of thousands of innocent nameless Afghan women, children, and men—victims of US bombings—went largely unpublicized.

Furthermore, September 11 had a terrible shock effect on the millions of Americans who get all their news from the corporate media and who were secure in the belief that everyone in the world secretly wants to be an American. They believed that America was universally loved and admired because the United States was more prosperous, nobler, and more generous than other countries. Very few Americans know about victims of US terrorism abroad. Relatively few are aware that whole societies have been shattered by US bombings or US monetary and trade policies. For instance, many are shocked—and skeptical—to hear that economic sanctions keep people in misery in Cuba and Iraq. Generally, they believe that US actions around the world have been benevolently motivated, dedicated to setting things right.

Then along came these 9/11 terrorists who had some education, looked like regular people, and actually lived in the United States and experienced this country firsthand. They could have applied for citizenship, but instead chose to commit mass murder and suicide to send us the message that we and our country, and what it represents, are horribly despised. What changed on September 11 was people's perception of themselves and of America's place in the world. Many felt shocked, smaller, not respected, less secure, less powerful, and confused. Some even wondered if there were things that they had not been told.

The entire nation and indeed the entire world knew about September 11 because of the repeated play it was given in the corporate-owned global media. In contrast, much of the world and almost all of America know next to nothing about how US supported terrorists have taken millions of lives in scores of other countries. The media have little to say about *those* acts of terrorism, and so the general public knows relatively little about them.[13]

A World Changed Forever?

In the aftermath of the attacks, President George II announced that "our nation can never go back to what it was on September 10." A tearful TV anchorman appeared on a late night show and blubbered about how this wound had changed America forever. The drumbeat carried across the political spectrum. A statement from the Communist Party, USA, issued in mid-November 2001 began: "Our world changed on September 11." And others wrote that "the indelible images of the World Trade Center will remain with us forever." A West Coast journalist claimed, "In a few minutes the world changed," and not just the world, "a universe [is] now lost."[14]

To be sure, the families and friends of the September 11 victims have had their lives changed drastically and tragically. But on the larger scene very little has really changed—unfortunately. Five months *before* the attacks, when the World Trade Center still stood tall, President Bush and the Congress hit us with a huge regressive $1.35 trillion tax cut that favored wealthy interests over everyone else. Then, in this post-September 11 world, before the dust had settled on ground zero in lower Manhattan, Bush was at it again, proposing an additional $160 billion in tax cuts mostly for big corporations and the very affluent. The world may have changed, but he was up to his same old tricks.

Just as in earlier times, the White House pushed for an "economic stimulus" package, consisting mostly of the usual corporate giveaways, bailouts, and retroactive tax cuts, all designed to help little struggling businesses like International Business Machines (IBM), Ford, General Motors, General Electric, and Chevron Texaco, while doing nothing for the tens of thousands of workers who have been laid off. IBM would get $1.4 billion, GM would pocket $833 million, and GE would make do with $671 million.[15] This caused Citizens for Tax Justice, a public interest group, to issue a broadside that began: "What's General Electric doing at this time of national tragedy? Profiteering in the name of patriotism." Again, there is something painfully familiar about all this. Business profiteering in the name of patriotism has occurred in every war this nation has fought.

Supposedly giveaways to corporations stimulate the economy. Given more money, the big companies invest more, create more jobs and more buying power, thereby ending the recession, or so we are told. But many of these companies are already wallowing in cash. And many of them suffer not from inadequate investment funds but from overcapacity. They are given billions in subsidies but they still lay off workers or do not hire back the ones they have downsized when demand is lagging. The problem is not a lack of capital among the superrich but insufficient consumer response, too many giant producers with too much wealth producing too many goods and services that underpaid or unemployed workers cannot afford to buy. To bolster the economy, public funds should be going into public job programs to augment the spending power of those most in need.

Instead, the fundamentalist free-market fanatics who run Washington continue to push in the opposite direction. In October 2001, a Republican-led Senate filibuster defeated legislation that would have stimulated the sagging economy by providing immediate aid to tens of thousands of downsized airline workers. House Majority Leader Dick Armey (R-Tex.), who has supported every corporate bailout and giveaway in sight, proclaimed that "it wouldn't be commensurate with the American spirit" to provide emergency aid to downsized airline workers.[16] All in all, here was a national leadership shamelessly *un*changed by the terrorist attacks.

After September 11, thousands of working people from New York and all over the country rushed to volunteer at the site of the disaster in lower Manhattan. Tens of thousands of others lined up to give blood or send donations totaling over $1 billion (much of it subsequently misspent—another familiar story). Some businesses also made contributions.

But Wall Street and the giant transnationals struck a more familiarly self-interested course. As Arthur Perlo observed, mutual fund managers and other financial experts urged people to invest in the stock market, being more concerned that money be contributed into their sagging investment funds than into needy relief funds. As a demonstration of their patriotic support, some ordinary citizens did withdraw money from their savings accounts and invested in the market. But the very rich were doing something else, demonstrating as always that their first loyalty was to their money. Perlo quotes Maria Lagomasino, head of the private banking division of JP Morgan that manages the fortunes of families with an average wealth of $100 million. She counseled her clients against getting back into the stock market. "Since our clients were rich, our number one concern was their staying rich," she cheerily admitted. Likewise, the *New York Times* reported, "Clients with a lot of their wealth in cash were cautioned against rushing back into the markets."[17]

But some stocks were worth rushing back into. Companies that marketed security services, bomb detection devices, and surveillance and biowarfare technologies rocketed up 146 percent after September 11, as did a number of defense contractors.[18]

Other things in the newly "transformed" America seem drearily familiar. A compliant Congress pumped billions more into an already bloated military budget. As in previous decades, our fearless leaders continued to wage devastatingly one-sided aerial wars against small, weak, impoverished nations, this time Afghanistan, while loading the media with jingoistic hype. They continued to send aid to a reactionary Likud-dominated coalition government in Israel so that it might go on battering the Palestinians—another policy that fails to endear us to the Muslim world.

Just as they did during the Clinton administration, lawmakers devised anti-terrorism bills that contained little to discourage real terrorists but much to terrorize civil libertarians and political dissenters. At the Senate hearings in mid December 2001, Attorney General John Ashcroft questioned the patriotism of those speaking out for civil liberties: "Your tactics only aid terrorists, for they erode our national unity and diminish our resolve. They give ammunition to America's enemies and pause to America's friends."[19] Substitute "communist" for "terrorist" in that statement and you have Senator Joe McCarthy conducting his witchhunt of half a century ago.

It was reported that the FBI was weighing the "torture option." Becoming increasingly frustrated by the silence of jailed suspects allegedly associated with the al Qaeda network, Justice Department investigators were openly thinking of resorting to more coercive methods of interrogation, using drugs or "pressure tactics," or transporting suspects to "allied countries where security services sometimes employ threats to family members or resort to torture."[20] But even this is nothing new. For years, the Justice Department and the Immigration and Naturalization Service have been deporting political refugees back to El Salvador, Guatemala, and other quasi-fascist regimes to be tortured or disappeared. And many of the torturers in the "security services" abroad have been trained and financed by the US national security state.

Even before September 11, there already were enough repressive laws on the books to round up all and sundry, be they citizens or not. The only thing that keeps the authorities from doing so is the fear that it might cause too much of a political uproar. Were resistance to heat up enough, were popular forces to mobilize and gather troublesome visibility and strength, then the powers that be might be tempted to employ more thorough applications of oppression.

"Free Trade" against Terrorism?

Both before and after September 11, the ruling elites persisted in pushing their brand of globalization with a fast track provision that would allow the president to railroad FTAA and other such "free trade" agreements through Congress without amendment or significant debate. US Trade representative Robert Zoellick, a member of the Bush Cabinet, enlisted the terrorism hype in the White House's campaign to surrender our democratic sovereignty to international trade councils. Zoellick charged that opposition to fast track and globalization was akin to supporting the terrorists.[21] House Republican leaders made similar assertions. Here was yet another opportunistic attempt to wrap the flag around a reactionary special interest.

Actually it is the free trade agreements that threaten our democratic sovereignty. Under agreements like NAFTA, GATT, GATS, and FTAA all public programs and services that regulate or infringe in any way upon big-money corporate capitalism can be rolled back by trade councils staffed by corporate personnel, elected by no one, unhampered by any conflict-of-interest laws. Corporations are able to tell governments (soon this will include local governments as well as state and federal) what public programs and regulations are acceptable or unacceptable. The reactionaries do not really explain how we fight terrorism by giving private, nonelective, corporate-dominated trade councils a supranational supreme power to override our laws and our Constitution.

As always, media pundits presented globalization as a natural, inevitable, and benign historical development. They told us that the world's economies have grown from local to regional to national to international modes of production and exchange, and now it was time for just one big happy *global* economy that would benefit everyone.

There is another view of globalization, the one that says it is neither natural nor beneficial to the peoples of the world; rather it is a subterfuge devised to benefit the rich investors of all nations at the expense of working people everywhere. If allowed to pass FTAA will remove all obstacles to the privatization of publicly funded services, including health, water, electricity, education, senior assistance, and environmental programs throughout the Western hemisphere. It will strip away every safeguard that workers have in protecting their living standards, including their right to have an input into such public policies.

The anti-globalization proponents correctly see that the various "free trade" agreements (a) circumvent democratic regulations that protect consumers, workers, and the environment, (b) move toward the elimination of public services (except police and military, and subsidies to big business), (c) force profit-making privatization upon all spheres of public life, and most important (d) undermine our very democratic right to have laws and services outside the veto power of nonelective trade councils dominated by the transnational corporations. Needless to say, those who see globalization as an attack upon democracy itself win no exposure in the major broadcast media.[22]

Still other things make our world seem very much as it was on September 10. As during every national crisis, liberal legislators supinely line up with conservatives to vote the president absolutist powers. Media lapdogs yelp about how this same president has "risen to the challenge" and "grown in office." One pundit even compared almost-elected George W. Bush to Abraham Lincoln.[23] Flag-waving yahoos call for blood, believing with all their hearts that their government only opposes terrorism and never practices it. Meanwhile, thousands of US residents— this time of Middle East origin—are subjected to racial profiling. African-American communities continue to be terrorized by trigger-happy cops. And fanatical Christian fundamentalists commit terrorist acts against abortion clinics while law officials seem unable to stop them. In a word, the world has not changed since September 11, certainly not for the better. The need to inject reality and justice into an impoverished national dialogue is as urgent as ever.

3   WHY DID IT HAPPEN?

WHY DID ISLAMIC EXTREMISTS ATTACK the World Trade Center and the Pentagon on September 11, 2001, taking the lives of thousands of innocent people? As the White House and corporate media would have it, they were crazed zealots driven by an evil doctrine. And they targeted the United States because it is such a free and prosperous country.

Killing for God and Country

As far as we can tell, the perpetrators were indeed propelled by the fanatical conviction that they were operating directly under God's command. There is an age-old relationship between religion and violence. Some observers try to explain away the connection as an aberration, an outside infection by a deviant ideology, a mutant extremist strain of religion. But in fact, the histories of Christianity, Judaism, Hinduism, and Islam, are tragically laced with violence and intolerance, a willingness to suppress and kill for the glory of God. "Within the histories of religious traditions— from biblical wars to crusading ventures and great acts of martyrdom—violence has lurked as a shadowy presence," notes Mark Juergensmeyer. "Images of death have never been far from the heart of religion's power to stir the imagination. . . . [R]eligion seem[s] to need violence, and violence religion."[24]

Throughout the ages, religionists have claimed a divine mandate to do God's work on earth by delivering terror and death upon heretics and other sinners. Originating in nomadic or early agrarian theocratic societies, religious texts are full of violent narratives, whether it be Hindu mythology or the Bible or the Koran. When society is felt to be out of order and unjust, God sanctions war to set things right. Religious ideologies develop out of these "sacred" texts over time in various ways, and are today employed by mullahs, monks, and jihadists, or by neo-Nazi Christians in America.

Think of the Christian fundamentalists in our own country, such as those "soldiers of Christ" who bomb abortion clinics and who have killed several clinical workers and doctors. Think also of Timothy McVeigh, associated with a group calling itself "Christian Identity," who killed 168 innocent people in the Oklahoma City terrorist bombing of 1995. McVeigh was convinced he was striking a blow at the federal government and at the Jews, liberals, and other secularists who have dislodged white Christian America from its spiritual moorings.[25]

(We might note parenthetically that McVeigh's terrorism did not cause the US government to launch retaliatory air strikes against the Christian Identity encampment in Elohim City on the Oklahoma-Arkansas border, nor to attack the Montana militia units from which some of his sympathizers sprang. Nor did the Feds deem it necessary to round up Christian Identity members or various militiamen.)

Even Buddhism, enjoying the undeserved reputation of being a wholly pacifist religion, has produced warring sects of monks throughout much of Asia. In Sri Lanka, "where great battles in the name of Buddhism are part of Sinhalese history, acts of violence perpetrated by Sinhalese activists in the latter decades of the twentieth century have been supported by Buddhist monks."[26]

Islam, like other religions, is a source of love and peace for many people. The terrorists who act in its name are violating its precepts, we are told. But Muslim terrorists are part of another time-honored tradition, the tradition of violence that can be found in all major religions. In sum, we cannot divorce religion from the things that are done in its name. Just as we credit religion for its acts of mercy and charity, so might we credit it for the acts of terror and bloody murder it has inspired throughout the ages.

But why would the Islamic terrorists attack America in particular? It is true that the United States is a free and prosperous country, at least to some extent. Thanks to the struggles waged by generations of ordinary Americans against the forces of privilege and plutocracy over the last two centuries, we do have a greater degree of political freedom and economic well-being than found in other capitalist countries such as Argentina, Haiti, Indonesia, Mexico, Nigeria, and Zaire. As compared to much of the capitalist world, we enjoy a remarkable prosperity, albeit one that is steeply unequal in its distribution and becoming ever more so with each passing decade. As the *New York Times* recently reported, "For 30 years the gap between the richest Americans and everyone else has been growing so much that the level of inequality is higher than in any other industrialized nation."[27] Indeed, the political liberties and prosperity that the American people have been able to win, despite the ferocious opposition of the capitalist plutocracy, remain constantly under siege and under threat of reactionary rollback.

But it is one thing to assert that America is free and prosperous, comparatively speaking, and another to claim that this was the reason the terrorists targeted our country. Canada and a number of Scandinavian and Western European countries enjoy at least as much freedom and prosperity as the United States, yet their embassies, military headquarters, and trade centers have not been hit. And if it is America's "freedom" that the terrorists hate why did they attack the symbols of US economic and military domination, the World Trade Center and the Pentagon, rather than, say, the Statue of Liberty?[28] Perhaps the target was not US freedom and democracy but Washington's record of support for exactly the opposite things: military and economic terrorism, autocracy, and mass destruction of civilian populations.

In other words, the standard explanation for why September 11 happened is grossly incomplete. For it leaves untouched the role played by US leaders in creating the inequality and exploitation that is the common fate of so much of the world, including the Middle East. It leaves unmentioned the successive acts of mass terrorism perpetrated by US leaders against peoples all over the globe. It treats "terrorism" only as something that others do to us.

Conditional Causes

The September 11 attacks were so horrifying and heart-less, so maniacal and cruel, that for a while they threat-ened to preempt all other concerns in public life. The transfixing images, reproduced without letup by the major media, had a telling impact on the public mind. So when almost-elected president George W. Bush called for the head of Osama bin Laden, the leader of an international terrorist organization suspected of having perpetrated the attacks, few voices in public life coun-seled restraint and sober reflection. In the style of a Wild West sheriff, Bush declared that he wanted bin Laden "dead or alive." Ostensibly in pursuit of that goal, he embarked upon a massive bombing campaign in Afghanistan that caused the deaths of additional thousands of innocent women, men and children.

Some of us who did not support the White House's massive aerial assault upon the people of Afghanistan have sought to contextualize the September attacks, noting that they did not come from nowhere but were related to a broader set of events. For suggesting that there were other causes to September 11 besides reli-gious fanaticism, we dissenters were accused of apolo-gizing for the terrorists and "blaming America." Sometimes we even were called "traitors" and "cow-ards." It reminded me of the way protestors were treated in the early days of the Vietnam war when many of us refused to suspend our critical perceptions and obediently rally around the flag.

To understand why some people opposed the latest US military intervention in the Middle East, I would suggest making a distinction between (a) the *immediate* cause, in this case, a coterie of fanatical evildoers driven by a deranged theology who killed thousands by plowing planeloads of innocent people into the World Trade Center and the Pentagon, and (b) an underlying set of *conditional* causes, specifically the backlog of exploitation and injustice that Western leaders and investors have delivered upon other peoples, and the role of the US national security state as a prime purveyor of poverty, injustice, and repression in the Middle East and other regions of the world. A consideration of conditional causes is not meant as an excuse to dismiss the immediate cause.

Bush's declaration, "Either you are with me or against me," is intended to suggest that if you oppose the White House policy, you are running with the terrorists. Those who accept Bush's assertion readily misread the dissenting position. Like their leader, they have difficulty holding two thoughts in their heads at the same time, specifically that one can abhor the terrorist attacks while also fixing blame on a wide array of factors that go beyond—*but include*—the terrorists themselves.

Why Do They Hate Us?

Asking why there are people around the world who hate us, the writer Madison Shockley offered a list of grievances: "Arrogance, dominance, exploitation, oppression, racism, militarism, imperialism. Shall I go on? . . . As long as we continue to thwart the aspirations for freedom and dignity for much of the Third World, there will be those who resent us, and some who hate us."[29] Similarly, a retired lieutenant-colonel of the US Air Force, Robert Bowman, argues that the United States was targeted not because it stands for freedom and human rights but because it stands "for dictatorship, bondage, and human exploitation in the world. We are the target of terrorists because we are hated. And we are hated because our government has done hateful things."[30]

Some 1.5 billion people in the world live in absolute economic desperation, lacking even basic food, shelter, and clean water. One-fifth of all young men in the Middle East are unemployed, and the region's per capita income is about $2100 yearly, according to the World Bank, which is prone to understate the levels of economic deprivation. Leading the other rich industrial nations, the United States "has for decades imposed poverty-generating policies that force states to privatize resources and slash public spending."[31] This increases unemployment and leads to greater poverty, disease, forced migration, and environmental devastation. In Egypt—home of Mohammed Atta, who piloted the first jet into the World Trade Center—8.5 percent of the children die before age five, while Egypt's government spends a mere 4 percent of its budget on health care.[32]

US power supports retrograde rightwing governments that are dedicated not to the well-being of their peoples but to servicing the transnational corporations and the US national security state. Many Third World leaders eagerly incur huge debts with the International Monetary Fund (IMF) and Western banks, then often pocket substantial chunks of the incoming loans. Scores of maldeveloped capitalist countries in the Third World are trapped in a deepening cycle of borrowing and repayment at usurious rates, a process that further enriches global financial interests at the expense of Third World populations. Over the past seventeen years, poor capitalist nations have transferred a net total of $1.5 trillion to rich foreign creditors.[33]

The deepening impoverishment that besets these debtor countries fuels popular resentment and rebellion. Leftist groups emerge and begin to mobilize large sectors of the population in the struggle for social betterment and against the economic servitude imposed by Western interests. These democratic movements are crushed by domestic military forces funded and advised by the US national security state. In some countries—Afghanistan is a prime example—the CIA employed rightwing fundamentalists to lead the assault against godless secular reformism and materialistic communism. "With the left defeated, malignant strains of Islamic fundamentalism are now filling the vacuum, offering a totalizing religious solution to everyday problems of privation and repression."[34]

Turkey provides another example. Progressive forces in that country have been subjected to an unsparing, US-supported repression for more than a half century. Hundreds of thousands of peasants, workers, students, teachers, and others have been incarcerated. Thousands have been tortured and executed, including hundreds of labor union leaders. Peasant cooperatives have been banned. In the 1980s, the US-supported rightwing government outlawed all popular and progressive political parties, abolished collective bargaining, froze or rolled back wages, eliminated benefits, and muzzled the press. Meanwhile, CIA-funded rightwing groups in Turkey gathered strength.[35]

Turkey today remains a police state with parliamentary window-dressing. Striving to preserve a secular society, the ruling elite has banned Islamic political parties. Bereft of their own popular organizations, the urban poor in Turkey now turn to these same parties, whose ranks are swelling despite the ban.[36]

Pakistan too bears witness to how Middle East terrorism is rooted in Western imperialism. As in so many other countries, in Pakistan structural adjustment programs (SAPs) imposed by the IMF roll back public subsidies, abolish price controls, freeze wages, and open domestic markets to transnational penetration. The SAPs have had a crippling effect on the economy, greatly exacerbating the already widespread poverty and underemployment. Meanwhile, sectarian violence and drug lords are tearing the social fabric to pieces. The terrorist training centers, set up in Pakistan in the early 1980s ostensibly to fight the Soviets in Afghanistan, have produced Islamic true-believers with much popular appeal within Pakistan itself.[37]

A regular spokesperson for the US foreign policy establishment, Fareed Zakaria, offers a surprisingly critical account of developments in the Middle East. Allowing that almost every Arab country "is less free than it was thirty years ago," Zakaria describes how young Arab men, often better educated than their elders, depart their villages to seek work and "arrive in noisy, crowded cites like Cairo, Beirut, and Damascus," where "they see great disparities of wealth and the disorienting effects of modernity." They witness unveiled women eating in cafés, children begging in streets, and everywhere the crass glitter of Western secular materialism, little of which they can themselves acquire. Both attracted and repelled by it all, frustrated and resentful, denied all democratic outlets for protest and change, these alienated youth move toward a resurgent militant Islam.[38]

"Blaming America"

Osama bin Laden repeatedly designated "America, Americans, and Jews" as the enemies to be eradicated. As a rich reactionary religious fanatic, bin Laden was doing what other reactionaries around the world have often done. He harnessed the legitimate grievances that people have felt regarding the conditions of their lives and directed them toward irrelevant foes.

This is what Hitler did with the Germans, channeling their grievances about unemployment, inflation, and poverty toward irrelevant enemies. Instead of pointing the finger at the rich German cartels that were plundering the land and labor of the German people, Hitler directed popular anger at the Versailles Allies, the Weimar Republic, the trade unions, the Communists, and lurking behind them all, the diabolical Jews. Now we have another fanatical rightwing ideologue, Osama bin Laden, doing much the same.

Truth is, it is not America as such that is to blame. This entity called "America" is a diverse and enormous country of 281 million people, almost all of whom had no hand in the events leading up to September 11. Few ordinary Americans ever demanded that US leaders pursue a course of force and violence to advance the global interests of rich investors. Americans, as such, are not to blame, and certainly not the Jews, despite what Hitler and bin Laden and dozens of other deranged bigots and zealots have imagined. Instead, we might cast a critical eye upon the policies of the US leadership in the service of reactionary interests at home and abroad, a subject to be pursued further in the next two chapters.

Some *Christian* rightwing fundamentalists also blame America. Soon after the attack on the World Trade Center, the reactionary Christian evangelist Jerry Falwell appeared on Pat Robertson's "The 700 Club," on the Christian Broadcasting Network (CBN). Falwell charged that abortion rights proponents, civil liberties groups, gay rights advocates, and feminists "helped this happen." He suggested that the September 11 assault might seem "minuscule" one day "if God continues to lift the curtain and allow the enemies of America to give us probably what we deserve." Sounding like bin Laden himself, Falwell charged that "God will not be mocked." At fault were "the pagans and the abortionists and the feminists and the gays and the lesbians. I point the finger at you and say, 'You made this happen.'"[39] Pat Robertson, himself another rightwing religious reactionary, eagerly chimed in, "Well, I totally concur. . . . Jerry, that's my feeling. I think we've just seen the antechamber to terror. We haven't even begun to see what they can do to the major population."

Here was a remarkable development. Christians and Muslims have been killing each other for centuries, and are still killing each other today, from Nigeria to the Philippines. But on US television two proselytizing reactionary Christian zealots seemed to be in agreement with proselytizing reactionary Islamic zealots who say that the corrupt liberalities and venalities of American society invite divine retribution. God certainly does work his wonders in mysterious ways.

A few days later, realizing that his remarks did not sit well with the general public, Falwell hastened to apologize for excoriating fellow Americans. Robertson, in turn, wiggled furiously away from both Falwell's words and his own, calling his guest's remarks "totally inappropriate" and "frankly, not fully understood" by himself or the show's other hosts.[40]

Various critics of US policy end up blaming America for the wars pursued in its name, noting that "all of us" have failed to stop what is being done in our name.[41] But does this mean we are collaborative authors of US militaristic policies? More often, we are kept in the dark about what is done in our name. I do not blame the American people for what fundamentalist Muslim zealots did on September 11, nor for what secretive and deceptive fundamentalist empire-building zealots in Washington have been doing to help create the kind of world that brought forth the religious zealots.

Part of the problem may lie in the bad habit that many people have in using "we" when they mean US political and financial elites. To say that "we" are thwarting democracy abroad, impoverishing other populations, or bombing innocent people, when really referring to the actions of the White House, the CIA, the Pentagon, the IMF and the WTO, is to assume a community of interest between the general public and those who regularly prey upon it, which is just what the predators want.

Using "we" when really meaning "they" also deprives us of using "we" when we really mean the general public or at least the dissenters from orthodox policy. It keeps us from recognizing the distinct interest we have in opposing those who pretend to rule in our name. Sometimes both usages of "we" can appear in the same sentence, and it begins to get ludicrous. I heard one progressive speaker say, "We have to organize and protest against what we are doing in Central America."

There is no denying that after September 11 millions supported the US military assault upon Afghanistan, for they were led to believe that this would stop terrorism and protect lives. As of December 2001, President

George II sported an 86 percent approval rating—up from a pallid 44 percent in pre-September days.[42] Still, there were millions of other Americans who, though deeply disturbed by the terrible deeds of September 11 and apprehensive about future attacks, were not swept up in the reactionary tide. If anything, tens of thousands of us have long remonstrated and demonstrated against the kind of policies currently pursued by the White House. *We* took to the streets not to hail the chief but to oppose his war and his reactionary agenda.

Significant numbers in labor, civil rights, civil liberties, and peace groups opposed the bombing of Afghanistan. A poll conducted by the Pew Research Center for People and the Press found that despite the endless media barrage 39 percent of African Americans and 17 percent of whites were doubtful about taking a military course of action.[43] Some major organizations came out against the bombing, such as the National Council of Churches and the American Public Health Association. Others, like the US Catholic Bishops Conference, at least raised serious questions about it. A mid-November survey showed that support for military action, while remaining strong, was cooling off, with larger numbers registering in the "mixed feelings" category.[44]

Opinion polls also indicated that when alternatives to war, such as extradition and trial of the perpetrators, were suggested, support for the bombings in Afghanistan dropped markedly. Even though US officials and media commentators have said next to nothing about utilizing international law and diplomacy, 30 percent of Americans support that option, compared to 54 percent who support military action (with 16 percent undecided) according to an October Gallup poll. Quite likely a majority of Americans would prefer an international law approach if they had ever heard it explained and discussed.

As images of Afghan civilian casualties came across the screen, support for the war began to wane, as also happened with the bombing campaign against Yugoslavia in 1999. CNN chairperson Walter Isaacson issued orders to his correspondents that when they broadcasted reports with footage of civilian deaths, hunger, and devastation they were to remind viewers that the Taliban harbored terrorists who killed thousands of Americans in September, as if viewers weren't being reminded almost every hour of every day by the media. Isaacson called it "perverse to focus too much on the casualties or hardship in Afghanistan."[45]

To save us from such perversity, the Pentagon bought the rights to all pictures of Afghanistan and nearby countries taken by the world's best commercial imaging satellite, Space Imaging Inc., at a cost of $1.9 million a month, plus additional fees of hundreds of thousands of dollars for the images it actually purchased. The Pentagon contract meant that news media and other organizations outside government would not be able to obtain their own high-resolution satellite images of the Afghan conflict or of the entire region.[46]

Pictures of killed or suffering Afghani civilians soon disappeared from the US news. We now could see nothing about the war except what the Pentagon wanted us to see, specifically, repetitive accounts about the search for bin Laden, admiring accounts of weapons capability, "war images that resemble video games," and footage of happy Afghans who, now liberated from the Taliban yoke, are trimming their beards or playing music.[47]

Rather than blaming America, I would say that many Americans are taken in by the various opinion molders who run the corporate media and the government. We are not the perpetrators of the empire's crimes abroad, rather we number among the victims. We suffer the enormous tax burdens that empire imposes, and the commensurate neglect of domestic needs. And along with the rest of the world, we are the targets of the deceptions perpetrated in its name.

But when given half a chance and some exposure to alternative information, millions of people in the United States are capable of falling out of step with the White House's commands—which is why such tight control is exercised over the communication universe. Millions want neither protracted wars nor a surrender of individual rights and liberties.

Even among the flag-wavers, support for Bush seems to be a mile wide and an inch deep. The media-hyped jingoistic craze that gripped the United States after September 11 was mostly just that, a craze. In time, the patriotic hype recedes and reality returns. One cannot pay the grocery bills with flags or pay the rent with vengeful slogans. Indeed, a December poll showed that respondents "are eager for the government to pay attention to domestic issues," and stop neglecting the economy and giving "too little attention to health care."[48] Other surveys indicate that the US public is not prepared to support the bombing of country after country.

My thoughts go back to another President Bush, George I, who—as he pursued his merciless aerial assault against the people of Iraq early in 1991—won an approval rating of 93 percent and a fawning resolution from Congress hailing his "unerring leadership." Yet within the year, he was soundly defeated for reelection by a garrulous governor from Arkansas, who himself was nothing to brag about.

4   AFGHANISTAN, THE UNTOLD STORY

LESS THAN A MONTH AFTER THE September 11 attacks, US leaders began an all-out aerial assault upon Afghanistan, the country harboring Osama bin Laden and his al Qaeda terrorist organization. At the time, little was said about the more than twenty years of US intervention in Afghanistan that had helped create Osama bin Laden and the very Taliban regime that US military forces now set about to destroy.

All we usually hear about Afghanistan's history is that in 1980 the United States intervened to stop a Soviet "invasion" in that country. Even many would-be progressives, who normally take a more critical view of US policy abroad, treat the US intervention against the

Soviet-supported government as "a good thing."[49] The real story is not such a good thing.

Some Real History

For generations, the great majority of Afghanistan's people were involved in farming. The landholding system had remained unchanged since feudal times, with more than 75 percent of the land owned by big landlords who comprised only 3 percent of the rural population. In the mid-1960s, democratic revolutionary elements coalesced to form the People's Democratic Party (PDP). In 1973, the king was deposed, but the government that replaced him proved to be autocratic, corrupt, and unpopular. It was forced out in 1978 after a massive demonstration in front of the presidential palace, and after the army intervened on the side of the demonstrators.

The military officers who took charge then invited the PDP to form a new government under the leadership of Noor Mohammed Taraki, a poet and novelist. This is how a Marxist-led coalition of national democratic forces came into office. "It was a totally indigenous happening. Not even the CIA blamed the USSR for it," writes John Ryan, a retired professor at the University of Winnipeg, who was conducting an agricultural research project in Afghanistan at about that time.

The new government began to pursue much needed reforms. It legalized labor unions, and set up a minimum wage, a progressive income tax, a literacy campaign, and programs that gave ordinary people greater access to health care, housing, and public sanitation. The Taraki government also continued a campaign begun by the king to emancipate women from their age-old tribal bondage. It provided public education for girls and for the children of various tribes. And it moved to eradicate the cultivation of opium poppy. Until then Afghanistan had been producing more than 70 percent of the world's opium used to make heroin.[50]

The government also abolished all debts owed by farmers, and began developing a major land reform program. Ryan believes that it was a "genuinely popular government and people looked forward to the future with great hope." However, serious opposition arose from several quarters. The feudal landlords opposed the land reform program that infringed on their holdings while benefiting poor tenant farmers. And tribesmen and fundamentalist mullahs vehemently opposed the government's dedication to gender equality and the education of women and children.[51]

Because of its egalitarian economic policies the government also incurred the opposition of the US national security state. The Marxists were advocating the kind of equitable distribution of social resources that incurs the hatred and fear of the US ruling class and privileged classes everywhere. Almost immediately after the PDP coalition came to power, the CIA, assisted by Saudi and Pakistani military, launched a large scale intervention into Afghanistan on the side of the ousted feudal lords, reactionary tribal chieftains, mullahs, and opium traffickers.

A top official within the Taraki government was Hafizulla Amin, believed by many to have been recruited by the CIA during the several years he spent in the United States as a student. In September 1979, Amin seized state power in an armed coup. He executed Taraki, halted the reforms, and murdered, jailed, or exiled thousands of Taraki supporters as he moved toward establishing a fundamentalist Islamic state. But within two months, he was overthrown by PDP remnants including elements within the military.

It should be noted that all of this happened *before* the Soviet military intervention. Zbigniew Brzezinski, national security adviser under President Carter, publicly admitted, months before Soviet troops entered the country that the Carter administration was providing huge sums to Muslim extremists to subvert the reformist government.

In late 1979, the restored but seriously besieged PDP government asked Moscow to send a contingent of troops to help ward off the mujahideen (Islamic guerrilla fighters) and foreign mercenaries, all recruited, financed, and well-armed by the CIA. The Soviets already had been sending assistance for projects in mining, education, agriculture, and public health. Sending troops represented a commitment of a more serious and politically dangerous sort. It took repeated requests from Kabul before Moscow agreed to intervene militarily.

Referring to her two visits to Afghanistan in 1980-81 during the first years of Soviet intervention, Marilyn Bechtel, former editor of *New World Review*, reported seeing women working together in handicraft co-ops; for the first time they were paid decently for their work and could control the money they earned. She observed women and men learning to read, and women working as professionals, holding responsible government positions. For the first time, poor working families were able to afford a doctor and to send their children to school. Bechtel also mentions the cancellation of peasant debt and the start of land reform, fledgling peasant cooperatives, price controls and price reductions on some key foods, and aid to nomads interested in a settled life. She was less happy to observe the brutal results of attacks upon schools and teachers in rural areas by the CIA-backed mujahideen.[52]

A report in the *San Francisco Chronicle* notes that "Kabul was once a cosmopolitan city. Artists and hippies flocked to the capital. Women studied agriculture, engineering and business at the city's university. Afghan women held government jobs—in the 1980s, there were seven female members of parliament. Women drove cars, traveled and went on dates. Fifty percent of university students were women."[53] In keeping with the ideological self-censorship that characterizes the US press, at no time does this story point out that women were doing all these things during the reign of a Soviet-supported Marxist government.

Jihad and Taliban, CIA Style

The Soviet intervention was a golden opportunity for the CIA to escalate the tribal resistance into a holy war, an Islamic jihad against godless communism. The goal was not only to expel the infidels from Afghanistan but eventually to liberate the Muslim-majority areas of the Soviet Union. Over the years the United States and Saudi Arabia expended about $40 billion on the war in Afghanistan. The CIA and its allies recruited, supplied, and trained almost 100,000 radical mujahideen from forty Muslim countries including Pakistan, Saudi Arabia, Iran, Algeria, and Afghanistan itself.[54] Among those who answered the call was Saudi-born millionaire rightwinger Osama bin Laden and his cohorts.

After a long and unsuccessful war, the Soviets evacuated the country in February 1989. It is generally thought that the PDP Marxist government collapsed immediately after the Soviet departure. Actually, it retained enough popular support to fight on for another three years, outlasting the Soviet Union itself by a year. The USSR was overthrown in 1991, while the PDP government in Kabul, despite the unending onslaught of superior US weaponry, prevailed into 1992.

Upon taking over Afghanistan, the mujahideen fell to fighting among themselves. They ravaged the cities, terrorized civilian populations, looted, staged mass executions, closed schools, raped thousands of women and girls, and reduced half of Kabul to rubble. Amnesty International reported that the mujahideen used sexual assault as "a method of intimidating vanquished populations and rewarding soldiers."[55]

Ruling the country gangster-style and looking for lucrative sources of income, the tribes ordered farmers to plant opium poppy. The Pakistani ISI, a close junior partner to the CIA, set up hundreds of heroin laboratories across Afghanistan. "Within two years of the CIA's arrival, the Pakistan-Afghanistan borderland had become the biggest producer of heroin in the world, and the single biggest source of the heroin on American streets."[56]

In Afghanistan the United States was "unaware that it was financing a future war against itself," Arundhati

Roy reminds us.[57] Largely created and funded by the CIA, the mujahideen mercenaries now took on a life of their own. Hundreds of them returned home to Algeria, Chechnya, Kosovo, and Kashmir to carry on terrorist attacks in Allah's name against the purveyors of secular "corruption."

In 1993 came the first attack upon the World Trade Center. A van filled with explosives was detonated in the WTC's underground garage, killing six people and injuring over a thousand others. Most of the terrorists involved were mujahideen veterans of the Afghan war. In 1995, a ten-member group convicted of a plot to bomb the United Nations building and several other targets in New York was led by Sheik Omar Abdul Rahman, who had worked with the mujahideen in Afghanistan. Earlier Rahman had obtained a US visa from a CIA undercover agent, leading to speculation that he still had CIA links at the time of the plot.[58] Such undertakings demonstrated the multi-centered, quasi-autonomous nature of these terrorist cells, and their ability to inject themselves into Western society.

In Afghanistan, the triumphant chieftains continued their turf fights and their wanton rule. In 1994 US and Pakistani leaders decided to back a group that might end the civil strife and unite the country around a stable rightwing government. Such a government could also insure the safety of the Unocal oil pipeline that was being planned to run through Afghanistan.[59] Within a year, an extremist strain of Sunni Islam called the Taliban—heavily funded and advised by the ISI and the CIA and with the support of Islamic political parties in Pakistan—fought its way to power, taking over most of the country, luring many tribal chiefs into its fold with threats and bribes.

The Taliban promised to end the factional fighting, lawlessness, and banditry that was the mujahideen trademark. But some modes of violence did not cease. Suspected murderers and spies were executed monthly in the sports stadium, and those accused of thievery had the offending hand sliced off.[60] Like their reactionary Christian counterparts, the Taliban condemned forms of "immorality" that included premarital sex, adultery, and homosexuality. And like Christian fundamentalists, they advanced a strict and literal interpretation of holy Scripture. They also outlawed all music, theater, libraries, literature, secular education, and much scientific research, again just as the Christians did through much of their early history.[61]

The Taliban unleashed a religious reign of terror, imposing an even stricter interpretation of Muslim law than used by most of the Kabul clergy. All men were required to wear untrimmed beards and women had to wear the burqa which covered them from head to toe, including their faces. Persons who were slow to comply were dealt swift and severe punishment by the Ministry of Virtue. Women were to remain completely subservient to men, no matter how brutal the men might be. A woman who fled an abusive home or charged spousal abuse would herself be severely whipped by the theocratic authorities. Females could not appear in public unless accompanied by a close male relative. Women had to blacken their house windows so they could not be seen by passing strangers. They could no longer attend the public baths even though these had always been strictly segregated by gender. They were outlawed from social life, deprived of most forms of medical care, all levels of education, and any opportunity to work outside the home. Women who were deemed "immoral" were stoned to death, and widows guilty of adultery were buried alive.

None of this was of much concern to leaders in Washington who got along famously with the Taliban. As recently as 1999, the US government paid the entire annual salary of every single Taliban government official.[62] Not until October 2001, when President George II had to rally public opinion behind his bombing campaign in Afghanistan did he denounce the Taliban's oppression of women. His wife, Laura Bush, emerged overnight as a full-blown feminist to deliver a public address detailing some of the abuses committed against Afghan women.

If anything positive can be said about the Taliban, it is that they did put a stop to much of the looting, raping, and random killings that the mujahideen had practiced on a regular basis. In 2000 Taliban authorities also eradicated the cultivation of opium poppy throughout the areas under their control, an effort judged by a United Nations agency to have been nearly totally successful.[63] With the Taliban overthrown and a Western-selected mujahideen government reinstalled in Kabul by December 2001, opium poppy production in Afghanistan reportedly was expected to increase dramatically.[64]

Of the nineteen terrorists identified as part of the September 11 attacks in New York and Washington seven were identified as Saudis, one as an Egyptian, and one as from the United Emirates. As far as is known, not one was a Taliban, and not one was from Afghanistan or had ever visited that country. Yet it was Afghanistan that was targeted for massive bombing, ostensibly because Osama bin Laden and his al Qaeda associates were directing their war against the United States from there.

By the end of 2001, the Taliban and al Qaeda forces either were destroyed, or had switched sides, or had fled into Pakistan. This came after two and a half months of massive US air strikes with Cruise missiles, Stealth bombers, Tomahawks, daisy cutters and other anti-personnel bombs. According to a study by Marc

Herold, an economist at the University of New Hampshire, over 3,760 civilians were killed by the war, not including the indirect deaths caused by land minds, hunger, cold, and lack of water.[65] The aerial assaults and the war in general turned a few million Afghans into refugees. By the end of 2001, more than seven million out of an estimated population of twenty-two million were classified by aid organizations as being at "very high risk" of starvation. With the onset of winter scores of Afghans were already dying from cold and hunger every night.[66]

Riding into power on the strength of US aerial assaults was the "Northern Alliance," a discordant coalition of tribal warlords known for the criminal anarchy of their rule in pre-Taliban days. Amnesty International reported that during the US-sponsored war of 2001, both the Taliban militia and their mujahideen opponents were committing "grave abuses, including indiscriminate killings of civilians and ethnically targeted killings." Reports of summary executions of Taliban prisoners by the mujahideen continued coming in to the end of 2001. A statement by the Revolutionary Association of Women of Afghanistan (RAWA) applauded the Taliban defeat but cautioned the world about the criminal nature of some Northern Alliance contingents. RAWA called for a United Nations' peacekeeping force to safeguard the human rights of the Afghan people, a proposal that elicited no enthusiasm from US leaders or tribal warlords but seemed to win support from ordinary Afghans.[67]

The Holy Crusade for Oil and Gas

The swift collapse of the Taliban did not solve the problem of terrorism. For one thing, as of the end of 2001, Osama bin Laden was nowhere in sight. Having failed to catch him, US leaders now suggested that he didn't really matter much. The important thing was that his organization and base of operation had been shattered. Besides, he may already have been blown to pieces in the bombings, it was conjectured.

Indeed, bin Laden may not have been all that important. Along with fighting terrorism there were other compelling reasons that drew US power into Afghanistan. The Central Asian region is rich in oil and gas reserves. The US Department of Energy estimates that the Caspian basin holds 110 billion barrels, about three times the United States's own reserves. And Turkmenistan has immense natural gas supplies. Hence it should come as no surprise that US policy elites were contemplating a military presence in Central Asia long before September 2001.[68] The discovery of vast oil and gas reserves in Kazakhstan and Turkmenistan provided the lure, while the dissolution of the USSR removed the

one major barrier against pursuing an aggressive inter-
ventionist policy in that part of the world.

US oil companies acquired the rights to some 75 percent of these new reserves. A major problem was how
to extract the oil and gas from the landlocked region.
US officials opposed using the Russian pipeline or the
most direct route across Iran to the Persian Gulf.
Instead, they and the corporate oil contractors explored
a number of alternative pipeline routes, across
Azerbaijan and Turkey to the Mediterranean or across
China to the Pacific. The one favored by Unocal, a US-
based oil company, crossed Afghanistan and Pakistan to
the Indian Ocean. The intensive negotiations that
Unocal entered into with the Taliban regime were still
unresolved by 1998, as an Argentine company placed a
competing bid for the pipeline. Bush's war against the
Taliban rekindled Unocal's hopes for getting a major
piece of the action.[69]

Interestingly enough, neither the Clinton nor Bush
administrations ever placed Afghanistan on the official
State Department list of states charged with sponsoring
terrorism, despite the acknowledged presence of
Osama bin Laden as a guest of the Taliban government.
Such a "rogue state" designation would have made it
impossible for a US oil or construction company to
enter an agreement with Kabul for a pipeline to the
Central Asian oil and gas fields.

In sum, the US government had made preparations well in advance of September 2001 to move against the Taliban and create a compliant regime in Kabul and a direct US military presence in Central Asia. The September 11 attacks provided the perfect impetus, stampeding US public opinion and reluctant allies into supporting military intervention.

Did They Know Ahead of Time?

The September terrorist attacks created such a service-able pretext for reactionism at home and imperialist expansion abroad as to leave many people suspecting that the US government itself had a hand in the event. A historical parallel is the charge made that President Franklin Delano Roosevelt was aware that Pearl Harbor was going to happen and did nothing to stop it because he wanted a casus belli that would galvanize a reluctant US public into entering World War II. There is no doubt that Roosevelt did indeed desire some way to shift public opinion toward intervention against the Axis powers. There is even evidence that he fitted out a US vessel, the Lani Kai, with mounted guns so that it might qualify as a man-o-war, and sent it into Japanese infested waters in the southwest Pacific supposedly on a reconnaissance voyage, but one that was likely to prove sacrificial. An attack on a US man-o-war would have constituted an act of war by Japan against the United States.[70] But before the Lani Kai could meet its preordained fate, Japanese Imperial forces launched a vastly more destructive attack on Pearl Harbor.

There might be reason to believe that Roosevelt knew the Japanese were up to something in the eastern Pacific that fateful Sunday morning of December 7, 1941. But there is no reason to think he anticipated— let alone collaborated in or welcomed—the destruction of the entire US Pacific fleet and the death of 2500 Americans at Pearl Harbor. US Secretary of the Navy Knox relates that Roosevelt was a man of supreme self-confidence but there was one occasion when he was seriously rattled: "[O]n the afternoon of Pearl Harbor, I went to the White House and [Roosevelt] was in the Oval Office. When I went in he was seated at his desk and was as white as a sheet. He was visibly shaken. You know, I think he expected to get hit; but he did not expect to get hurt."[71]

I find it hard to believe that the White House or the CIA actively participated in a conspiracy to destroy the World Trade Center and part of the Pentagon, killing such large numbers of Americans in order to create a casus belli against Afghanistan. But this does not preclude the possibility that they expected *something* to happen and looked the other way—without anticipating the magnitude of the destruction.

Patrick Martin writes that immediately after the attacks, stories in the overseas press asserted that US intelligence agencies had received specific warnings about impending terrorist attacks, including the use of hijacked airplanes. Martin points to the strange decision by top FBI officials to block an investigation into Zaccarias Massaoui, the Franco-Moroccan immigrant who was arrested in early August after he allegedly sought training from a US flight school on how to steer a commercial airliner, but not to take off or land. The Minneapolis FBI field office asked FBI headquarters in Washington for permission to conduct further inquiries into Massaoui's doings. FBI chiefs refused on grounds that there was insufficient evidence of criminal intent—"an astonishing decision for an agency not known for its tenderness on the subject of civil liberties." Martin goes on: "This is not to say that the American government deliberately planned every detail of the terrorist attacks or anticipated that [thousands of] people would be killed. But the least likely explanation of September 11 is the official one: that dozens of Islamic fundamentalists, many with known ties to Osama bin Laden, were able to carry out a wide-ranging conspiracy on three continents, targeting the most prominent symbols of American power, without any US intelligence agency having the slightest idea of what they were doing."72

One might agree with John Ryan who argued that if Washington had left the Marxist Taraki government alone back in 1979, "there would have been no army of mujahideen, no Soviet intervention, no war that destroyed Afghanistan, no Osama bin Laden, and no September 11 tragedy."[73] But it would be asking too much for Washington to leave unmolested a progressive leftist government that was organizing the social capital around collective needs rather than private accumulation.

As I noted in an earlier book: US intervention in Afghanistan proved not much different from US intervention in Cambodia, Angola, Mozambique, Ethiopia, Nicaragua, and elsewhere. It had the same intent of preventing egalitarian social change, and the same effect of overthrowing an economically reformist government. In all these instances, the intervention brought retrograde elements into ascendance, left the economy in ruins, and pitilessly laid waste hundreds of thousands of lives.[74]

The war against Afghanistan, a weak battered impoverished country, was portrayed in US official circles as a gallant crusade against terrorism. If it was that, it also was something else—a means of mobilizing public opinion, gaining profitable control of the last vast untapped reserve of the earth's dwindling fossil fuel resources, creating another compliant puppet regime, and extending US power directly into still another region of the world.

5 WHY US LEADERS INTERVENE EVERYWHERE

WASHINGTON POLICYMAKERS CLAIM that US intervention is motivated by a desire to fight terrorism, bring democracy to other peoples, maintain peace and stability in various regions, defend our national security, protect weaker nations from aggressors, oppose tyranny, prevent genocide, and the like. But if US leaders have only the best intentions when they intervene in other lands, why has the United States become the most hated nation in the terrorist's pantheon of demons? And not only Muslim zealots but people from all walks of life around the world denounce the US government as the prime purveyor of violence and imperialist exploitation.[75] Do they see something that most Americans have not been allowed to see?

Supporting the Right

Since World War II, the US government has given some $240 billion in military aid to build up the military and internal security forces of more than eighty other nations. The purpose of this enormous effort has been not to defend these nations from invasion by foreign aggressors but to protect their various ruling oligarchs and multinational corporate investors from the dangers of domestic anticapitalist insurgency. That is what some of us have been arguing. But how can we determine that? By observing that (a) with few exceptions there is no evidence suggesting that these various regimes have ever been threatened by attack from neighboring countries; (b) just about all these "friendly" regimes have supported economic systems that are integrated into a global system of corporate domination, open to foreign penetration on terms that are singularly favorable to transnational investors; (c) there is a great deal of evidence that US-supported military and security forces and death squads in these various countries have been repeatedly used to destroy reformist movements, labor unions, peasant organizations, and popular insurgencies that advocate some kind of egalitarian redistributive politics for themselves.[76]

For decades we were told that a huge US military establishment was necessary to contain an expansionist world Communist movement with its headquarters in Moscow (or sometimes Beijing). But after the overthrow of the Soviet Union and other Eastern European communist nations in 1989-1991, Washington made no move to dismantle its costly and dangerous global military apparatus. All Cold War weapons programs continued in full force, with new ones being added all the time, including the outer-space National Missile Defense and other projects to militarize outer space. Immediately the White House and Pentagon began issuing jeremiads about a whole host of new enemies—for some unexplained reason previously overlooked—who menace the United States, including "dangerous rogue states" like Libya with its ragtag army of 50,000 and North Korea with its economy on the brink of collapse.

The real intentions of US national security state leaders can be revealed in part by noting whom they assist and whom they attack. US leaders have consistently supported rightist regimes and organizations and opposed leftist ones. The terms "Right" and "Left" are seldom specifically defined by policymakers or media commentators—and with good reason. To explicate the politico-economic content of leftist governments and movements is to reveal their egalitarian and usually democratic goals, making it much harder to demonize them. The "Left," as I would define it, encompasses those individuals, organizations, and governments that oppose the privileged interests of wealthy propertied classes, while advocating egalitarian redistributive policies and a common development beneficial to the general populace.

The Right too is involved in redistributive politics, but the distribution goes the other way, in an upward direction. Rightist governments and groups, including fascist ones, are dedicated to using the land, labor, markets, and natural resources of countries as so much fodder for the enrichment of the owning and investing classes. In almost every country including our own, rightist groups, parties, or governments pursue tax and spending programs, wage and investment practices, methods of police and military control, and deregulation and privatization policies that primarily benefit those who receive the bulk of their income from investments and property, at the expense of those who live off wages, salaries, fees, and pensions. That is what defines and distinguishes the Right from the Left.

In just about every instance, rightist forces are deemed by US opinion makers to be "friendly to the West," a coded term for "pro-capitalist." Conversely, leftist ones are labeled as "anti-democratic," "anti-

American" and "anti-West," when actually what they are against is global capitalism.

While claiming to be motivated by a dedication to human rights and democracy, US leaders have supported some of the most notorious rightwing autocracies in history, governments that have tortured, killed or otherwise maltreated large numbers of their citizens because of their dissenting political views, as in Turkey, Zaire, Chad, Pakistan, Morocco, Indonesia, Honduras, Peru, Colombia, Argentina, El Salvador, Guatemala, Haiti, the Philippines, Cuba (under Batista), Nicaragua (under Somoza), Iran (under the Shah), and Portugal (under Salazar).

Washington also assists counterrevolutionary groups that have perpetrated some of the most brutal bloodletting against civilian populations in leftist countries: Unita in Angola, Renamo in Mozambique, the contras in Nicaragua, the Khmer Rouge (during the 1980s) in Cambodia, the mujahideen and then the Taliban in Afghanistan, and the rightwing drug-dealing KLA terrorists in Kosovo. All this is a matter of public record although seldom if ever treated in the US media.

Washington's support has extended to the extreme rightist reaches of the political spectrum. Thus, after World War II US leaders and their Western capitalist allies did nothing to eradicate fascism from Europe, except for prosecuting some top Nazi leaders at

Nuremberg. In short time, former Nazis and their collaborators were back in the saddle in Germany. Hundreds of Nazi war criminals found a haven in the United States and Latin America, either living in comfortable anonymity or employed by US intelligence agencies during the Cold War.[77]

In France, very few Vichy collaborators were purged. "No one of any rank was seriously punished for his or her role in the roundup and deportation of Jews to Nazi camps."[78] US military authorities also restored fascist collaborators to power in various Far East nations. In South Korea, police trained by the fascist Japanese occupation force were used after the war to suppress left democratic forces. The South Korean Army was commanded by officers who had served in the Imperial Japanese Army, some of whom had been guilty of horrid war crimes in the Philippines and China.[79]

In Italy, within a year after the war, almost all Italian fascists were released from prison while hundreds of communists and other leftist partisans who had been valiantly fighting the Nazi occupation were jailed. Allied authorities initiated most of these measures.[80] In the three decades after the war, US government agencies gave an estimated $75 million to right-wing organizations in Italy. From 1969 to 1974, high-ranking elements in Italian military and civilian intelligence agencies, along with various secret and highly placed neofascist groups embarked upon a campaign of terror and sabotage known as the "strategy of tension," involving a series of kidnappings, assassinations, and bombing massacres directed against the growing popularity of the democratic parliamentary Left. In 1995, a deeply implicated CIA, refused to cooperate with an Italian parliamentary commission investigating this terrorist campaign.[81]

In the 1980s, scores of people were murdered in Germany, Belgium, and elsewhere in Western Europe by rightwing terrorists in the service of state security agencies. As with the earlier "strategy of tension" in Italy, the attacks attempted to create enough popular fear and uncertainty to undermine the existing social democracies. The US corporate-owned media largely ignored these events.

Attacking the Left

We can grasp the real intentions of US leaders by looking at who they target for attack, specifically just about all leftist governments, movements, and popular insurgencies. The methods used include (a) financing, infiltrating, and coopting their military, and their internal security units and intelligence agencies, providing them with police-state technology including instruments of torture; (b) imposing crippling economic sanctions and IMF austerity programs; (c) bribing political leaders, military leaders, and other key players; (d) inciting retrograde ethnic separatists and supremacists within the country; (e) subverting their democratic and popular organizations; (f) rigging their elections; and (g) financing collaborationist political parties, labor unions, academic researchers, journalists, religious groups, nongovernmental organizations, and various media.

US leaders profess a dedication to democracy. Yet over the past five decades, democratically elected reformist governments— "guilty" of introducing egalitarian redistributive economic programs in Guatemala, Guyana, the Dominican Republic, Brazil, Chile, Uruguay, Syria, Indonesia (under Sukarno), Greece, Cyprus, Argentina, Bolivia, Haiti, the Congo, and numerous other nations—were overthrown by their respective military forces funded and advised by the US national security state. The intent behind Washington's policy is seen in what the US-sponsored military rulers do when they come to power. They roll back any reforms and open their countries all the wider to foreign corporate investors on terms completely favorable to the investors.

The US national security state has participated in covert actions or proxy mercenary wars against reformist or revolutionary governments in Cuba,

Angola, Mozambique, Ethiopia, Portugal, Nicaragua, Cambodia, East Timor, Western Sahara, Egypt, Cambodia, Lebanon, Peru, Iran, Syria, Jamaica, South Yemen, the Fiji Islands, Afghanistan, and elsewhere. In many cases the attacks were terroristic in kind, directed at "soft targets" such as schools, farm cooperatives, health clinics, and whole villages. These wars of attrition extracted a grisly toll on human life and frequently forced the reformist or revolutionary government to discard its programs and submit to IMF dictates, after which the US-propelled terrorist attacks ceased.

Since World War II, US forces have invaded or launched aerial assaults against Vietnam, Laos, the Dominican Republic, North Korea, Cambodia, Lebanon, Grenada, Panama, Libya, Iraq, Somalia, Yugoslavia, and most recently Afghanistan—a record of direct military aggression unmatched by any communist government in history. US/NATO forces delivered round-the-clock terror bombings on Yugoslavia for two and a half months in 1999, targeting housing projects, private homes, hospitals, schools, state-owned factories, radio and television stations, government owned hotels, municipal power stations, water supply systems, and bridges, along with hundreds of other nonmilitary targets at great loss to civilian life. In some instances, neoimperialism has been replaced with an old-fashioned direct colonialist occupation, as in Bosnia,

Kosovo, and Macedonia where US troops are stationed, and more recently in Afghanistan.

In 2000-2001, US leaders were involved in a counterinsurgency war against leftist guerrilla movements in Colombia. They also were preparing the public for moves against Venezuela, whose president, Hugo Chavez, is engaged in developing a popular movement and reforms that favor the poor. Stories appearing in the US press tell us that Chavez is emotionally unstable, autocratic, and bringing his country to ruin, the same kind of media hit pieces that demonized the Sandinistas in Nicaragua, the New Jewel Movement in Grenada, Allende in Chile, Noriega in Panama, Qaddafi in Libya, Milosevic in Yugoslavia, and Aristide in Haiti, to name some of the countries that were subsequently attacked by US forces or surrogate mercenary units.

Governments that strive for any kind of economic independence, or apply some significant portion of their budgets to not-for-profit public services, are the ones most likely to feel the wrath of US intervention. The designated "enemy" can be (a) a *populist military government* as in Panama under Omar Torrijos (and even under Manuel Noriega), Egypt under Gamal Abdul Nasser, Peru under Juan Velasco, Portugal under the leftist military officers in the MFA, and Venezuela under Hugo Chavez; (b) a *Christian socialist government* as in Nicaragua under the Sandinistas; (c) a *social democracy* as in Chile under Salvador Allende, Jamaica under Michael Manley, Greece under Andreas Papandreou, Cyprus under Mihail Makarios, and the Dominican Republic under Juan Bosch; (d) an *anti-colonialist reform government* as in the Congo under Patrice Lumumba; (e) a *Marxist-Leninist government* as in Cuba, Vietnam, and North Korea; (f) an *Islamic revolutionary order* as in Libya under Omar Qaddafi; or even (g) a *conservative militarist regime* as in Iraq under Saddam Hussein if it should attempt an independent course on oil quotas and national development.

The goal of US global policy is the Third Worldization of the entire world including Europe and North America, a world in which capital rules supreme with no labor unions to speak of; no prosperous, literate, well-organized working class with rising expectations; no pension funds or medical plans or environmental, consumer, and occupational protections, or any of the other insufferable things that cut into profits.

While described as "anti-West" and "anti-American," just about all leftist governments—from Cuba to Vietnam to the late Soviet Union—have made friendly overtures and shown a willingness to establish normal diplomatic and economic relations with the United States. It was not their hostility toward the United States that caused conflict but Washington's intolerance of the alternative class systems they represented.

In the post-World War II era, US policymakers sent assistance to Third World nations, and put forth a Marshall plan, grudgingly accepting reforms that produced marginal benefits for the working classes of Western Europe and elsewhere. They did this because of the Cold War competition with the Soviet Union and the strong showing of Communist parties in Western European countries.[82] But today there is no competing lure; hence, Third World peoples (and working populations everywhere) are given little consideration in the ongoing campaigns to rollback the politico-economic democratic gains won by working people in various countries.

After the Counter-Revolution

One can judge the intentions of policymakers by the policies they pursue in countries that have been successfully drawn back into the Western orbit. Consider Grenada. In 1983, US forces invaded the tiny and relatively defenseless sovereign nation of Grenada (population 110,000) in blatant violation of international law. The Reagan administration justified the assault by claiming it was a rescue operation on behalf of American students whose safety was being threatened at the St. George medical school. The White House also asserted that the New Jewel revolutionary government had allowed the island to become a Soviet-Cuban training camp, harboring a large contingent of Cuban troops and "deadly armaments" "to export terror and undermine democracy." It was further charged that the New Jewel government was planning to build a Soviet submarine base and Soviet military air base that would use Grenada to control crucial "choke points" along oil tanker lanes that came to the United States, thereby bringing us to our knees.[83] When these charges proved to be without foundation,[84] some critics concluded that White House policy toward Grenada therefore had been unduly alarmist and misguided. But the fact that officials offer alarmist and misleading rationales is no reason to conclude ipso facto that they are themselves misled. It may be that they have other motives which they prefer not to enunciate.

Under the Grenadian revolutionary government, free milk and other foodstuffs were being distributed to the needy, as were materials for home improvement. Grade school and secondary education were free for everyone for the first time. Free health clinics were opened in the countryside, thanks mostly to assistance rendered by Cuban doctors. Measures were taken in support of equal pay and legal status for women. Unused land was leased to establish farm cooperatives and turned agriculture away from cash-crop exports and more toward self-sufficient food production.[85]

The US invasion and occupation put an end to almost all these programs. Under US hegemony, unemployment in Grenada reached new heights and poverty new depths. Domestic cooperatives were suppressed or starved out. Farm families were displaced to make way for golf courses, and the corporate controlled tourist industry boomed. Grenada was once more firmly bound to the privatized free-market world, once again safely Third Worldized.

The same process occurred after the US invaded Panama in December 1989, supposedly to bring Manuel Noriega, described as a drug-dealing dictator, to justice. With Noriega and his leftist military deposed and the US military firmly in control, conditions in Panama deteriorated sharply. Unemployment, already high because of the US embargo, climbed to 35 percent as drastic layoffs were imposed on the public sector. US occupation authorities eliminated pension rights and other work benefits, ended public sector subsidies, privatized public services, shut down publicly owned media, and jailed a number of Panamanian editors and reporters critical of the invasion. The US military arrested labor union leaders and removed some 150 local labor leaders from their elected positions within their unions. Crime, poverty, drug trafficking, and homelessness increased dramatically.[86] Free-market Third Worldization was firmly reinstated in Panama under the banner of "democracy."

The same reactionary pattern was discernible in Eastern Europe and the former Soviet Union. For decades we were told by US leaders, media commentators, and academic policy experts that the Cold War was a struggle against an expansionist world communism, with nothing said about the expansionist interests of world capitalism. But immediately after communism was overthrown in the USSR in 1991, US leaders began intimating that there was something more on their agenda than just free elections for the former "captive nations"—namely free markets. Getting rid of communism, it became clear, meant getting rid of public ownership of the means of production. Of what use was political democracy, they seemed to be saying, if it allowed the retention of an economy that was socialistic or even social democratic? So the kind of polity seemed to weigh less than the kind of economy. The goal was, and continues to be, totally privatized economies that favor rich investor interests at the expense of the people in these countries.

When Words Speak Louder than Actions

It should not go unnoticed that US leaders occasionally do verbalize their dedication to making the world safe for the transnational corporate system. At such times words seem to speak louder than actions, for the words are an admission of the real intention behind the action. For example, as President Woodrow Wilson contemplated sending US troops as part of the expeditionary force of Western nations to overthrow the newly installed revolutionary socialist government in Russia in 1917, his Secretary of State, Robert Lansing, recorded in a confidential memorandum the administration's class concerns. Lansing ignored all the blather that US leaders were publicly mouthing about Lenin and the Bolsheviks being German agents. Instead he perceived them to be revolutionary socialists who sought "to make the ignorant and incapable mass of humanity dominate the earth." The Bolsheviks wanted "to overthrow all existing governments and establish on the ruins a despotism of the proletariat in every country." Their appeal was to "a class which does not have property but hopes to obtain a share by process of government rather than by individual enterprise. This is of course a direct threat at existing social order [i.e., capitalism] in all countries." The danger was that it "may well appeal to the average man, who will not perceive the fundamental errors."[87]

Almost four decades later, in 1953, President Dwight Eisenhower uttered a forbidden truth in his State of the Union message: "A serious and explicit purpose of our foreign policy [is] the encouragement of a hospitable climate for [private] investment in foreign nations."[88]

In 1982, the elder George Bush, then vice-president in the Reagan administration, announced, "We want to maintain a favorable climate for foreign investment in the Caribbean region, not merely to protect the existing US investment there, but to encourage new investment opportunities in stable, democratic, free-market oriented countries close to our shores." Not only close to our shores but everywhere else, as, General Gray, commandant of the US Marines, observed in 1990, saying that the United States must have "unimpeded access" to "established and developing economic markets throughout the world."[89]

President Clinton announced before the United Nations on September 27, 1993: "Our overriding purpose is to expand and strengthen the world's community of market-based democracies."[90] And over the past decade US policymakers have repeatedly and explicitly demanded "free-market reforms" in one country after another in the former communist nations of Eastern Europe.

Far from being wedded to each other, as US leaders and opinion makers would have us believe, capitalism and democracy are often on a fatal collision course. US leaders find electoral democracy useful when it helps to destabilize one-party socialism and serves as a legitimating cloak for capitalist restoration. But when it becomes a barrier to an untrammeled capitalism, democracy runs into trouble. This was demonstrated when the US national security state overthrew popular democratic governments in Guatemala in 1953, Chile in 1973, Greece in 1967, Indonesia in 1965, and a score of other countries.

The most recent example is Yugoslavia. Multi-ethnic Yugoslavia was once a regional industrial power and economic success, with a high annual growth rate, free medical care, a literacy rate over 90 percent, and a relatively equitable and prosperous economic life for its various peoples. While Yugoslavia was not, after the 1970s, a strictly socialist country, US policymakers knew that the economy was still 75 percent publicly owned and still had a large and egalitarian public service sector that was out of line with the push toward free-market Third Worldization.

As early as 1984, the Reagan administration issued US National Security Decision Directive 133: "United States Policy towards Yugoslavia," labeled "secret sensitive." It followed closely the objectives laid out in an earlier directive aimed at Eastern Europe, one that called for a "quiet revolution" to overthrow Communist governments while "reintegrating the countries of Eastern Europe into the orbit of the World market" (that is, global capitalism). The economic "reforms" pressed upon Yugoslavia by the IMF and other foreign creditors mandated that all socially owned firms and all worker-managed production units be transformed into private capitalist enterprises. [91]

In February 1999, US officials at Rambouillet made their determined dedication to economic privatization perfectly clear. Chapter 4a, Article 1, of the Rambouillet "agreement," actually an ultimatum imposed upon what remained of Yugoslavia (Serbia and Montenegro), stated in no uncertain terms: "The economy of Kosovo shall function in accordance with free market principles." There was to be no restriction on the movement of "goods, services, and capital to Kosovo," and all matters of trade, investment and corporate ownership were to be left to the private market.[92]

In 2000, the "Stability Pact for Southeastern Europe," called for "creating vibrant market economies" in the Balkans. It was hailed by the Clinton administration for offering "advice on investment" to all the countries of Southeast Europe. That same year, the Overseas Private Investment Corporation (OPIC) inaugurated a fund to be managed by Soros Private Funds Management. Its purpose, as stated by the US embassy in Macedonia, is "to provide capital for new business development, expansion and privatization."[93] Meanwhile the Agency for International Development (USAID) announced its intention to undertake "assistance programs to support economic reform and restructuring the economy . . . to advance Montenegro toward a free market economy."[94]

Along with the words came the actions. A decade of IMF restructuring, years of US-led, boycott, embargo, wars of secession, and weeks of massive bombing in 1999 left the Yugoslav economy in ruins. In April 2001, according to the London *Financial Times*, the newly installed "pro-West" rulers of Yugoslavia, beneficiaries of millions of dollars in US electoral funds, launched "a comprehensive privatization program as part of economic reforms introduced following the overthrow of former president Slobodan Milosevic." This included the sale of more than 7,000 publicly owned or worker controlled companies to private investors.[95]

"Conspiracy," "Incompetence," and "Inertia"

All of us are expected to make plans and intentionally pursue certain goals in life, and we recognize that throughout history other nations have defined objectives that they have carried through with resolve. But when one suggests that the US national security state operates with foreordained intent, mainstream social scientists and media pundits dismiss such a notion as "conspiracy theory." Policies that produce unfortunate effects on others are explained away as "unintended consequences." Of course, unintended consequences do arise, and upheavals do sometimes catch US leaders off guard, but there is no reason to reduce so much of policy outcome to stochasticism, to argue that things almost always occur by chance; stuff just happens, as innocently befuddled leaders grope about unburdened by any preconceived agenda.

To say, as I do, that US national security leaders know more, intend more, and do more than they let on is not to claim they are omnipotent or omnicompetent. It is to argue that US policy is not habitually misguided and bungling, although mistakes are made and indeterminancies certainly arise. Generally, US foreign policy is remarkably consistent and cohesive, a deadly success, given the interests it represents.

Sometimes the policymakers themselves seize upon incompetence as a cover. In 1986 it was discovered that the Reagan administration was running a covert operation to bypass Congress (and the law), using funds from secret arms sales to Iran to finance counterrevolutionary mercenaries (the "contras") in Nicaragua and probably GOP electoral campaigns at home. President Reagan admitted full knowledge of the arms sales, but claimed he had no idea what happened to the money. He was asking us to believe that these operations were being conducted by subordinates, including his very own National Security Advisor, without being cleared by him. Reagan publicly criticized himself for his slipshod managerial style and lack of administrative control over his staff. His admission of incompetence was eagerly embraced by various commentators who prefer to see their leaders as suffering from innocent ignorance rather than to see deliberate deception. Subsequent sworn testimony by his subordinates, however, revealed that Reagan was not as dumb as he was pretending to be, and that he had played a deciding role in the entire Iran-contra affair.[96]

Throughout its history, the CIA and other agencies of the national security state have resorted to every conceivable crime and machination, using false propaganda, sabotage, bribery, rigged elections, collusion with organized crime, narcotics trafficking, death squads, terror bombings, torture, massacres, and wars of attrition. At the same time, US leaders have pretended to have had nothing to do with such things. No less a political personage than Henry Kissinger repeatedly pretended to ignorance and incompetence when confronted with the dirty role he and his cohorts played in East Timor, Indochina, Chile, Bangladesh, and elsewhere. Kissinger's writings and speeches are heavily larded with exhortations about the importance of maintaining the efficacy of US policy and the need to impress the world with the mettle of US resolve. "Yet in response to any inquiry that might implicate him in political crimes, he rushes to humiliate his own country and its professional servants, suggesting that they know little, care less, are poorly informed and easily rattled by the pace of events."[97]

Sometimes outcomes are explained away as the result of a disembodied organizational inertia. Interventions are said to occur because a national security agency wants to prove its usefulness or is simply carried along on its own organizational momentum, as supposedly happened with the CIA and Pentagon intervention in Cuba during the Bay of Pigs invasion in 1961. To be sure, organizational modes of operation do come into play, but to see them as the predominant force behind policies is like claiming that the horses are the cause of the horse race.

The "Other Variables" Argument

US leaders may be motivated by all sorts of concerns such as advancing their nation's prestige, maintaining national security against potentially competing capitalist nations, developing strategic military superiority, distracting the American public from domestic problems and scandals, advancing the heroic macho image of the president, and the like. But these purposes almost always dovetail with dominant capitalist interests, or certainly do not challenge those interests in any serious way. Thus, while a US president might be interested in promoting his macho image, he would never think of doing so by supporting the cause of socialist reformation in this or any other country.

That officeholders seek to achieve many other purposes, Ralph Miliband once noted, "should not obscure the fact that *in the service of these purposes*, they become the dedicated servants of their business and investing classes."[98] The point is not that nations act imperialistically for purely material motives but that in addition to other considerations, policymakers will not move against the system-sustaining material interests of the dominant corporate class.

In sum, when trying to understand the events of September 11 we need to remember that US politico-corporate elites have resorted to every conceivable subterfuge, coercion, and act of terrorist violence in their struggle to make the world safe for transnational corporate capital accumulation; to attain control of the markets, lands, natural resources, and cheap labor of all countries; and to prevent the emergence of revolutionary socialist, populist, or even nationalist regimes that challenge this arrangement by seeking to build alternative productive systems. The goal is to create a world populated by client states and compliant populations open to transnational corporate penetration on terms that are completely favorable to the penetrators. It is not too much to conclude that such a consistent and ruthless policy of global hegemony is produced not by dumb coincidence but by conscious design.

6   EPILOGUE: WHAT IS TO BE UNDONE?

US LEADERS HAVE YET TO EXPLAIN HOW the destruction of the Taliban or even the destruction of Osama bin Laden and his al Qaeda group in far off Afghanistan will stop longstanding terrorist cells that operate with a substantial degree of autonomy in the West. In time, the American people may catch wise that the reactionaries in the White House have done relatively little to protect the many vulnerable points in our industrial society from terrorist attack. It would take just one suicide pilot in a single engine plane loaded with dynamite to hit a nuclear plant, causing an explosion that could kill or sicken millions. It would take just one terrorist, using the right kind of biochemical materials, to contaminate a city reservoir or the feedlot of a large herd of cattle, causing illness and death of epidemic proportions. Of 16,000 containers a day that arrive in our ports, only 500 are inspected. Even a former member of the Reagan defense establishment complains about the lack of security, noting that in 2002 the Pentagon will spend more on National Missile Defense (son of Star Wars) than on the Coast Guard.[99]

And what of the longterm conditions that foster terrorism? Here too, US leaders seem more interested in taking advantage of terrorist attacks than in preventing the conditions that breed them. They have neither the interest nor the will to make the kind of major changes in policy needed to dilute the hatred that so many people around the world feel toward US power. For one thing, they have no interest in breaking the "cycle of violence" by refraining from massive aerial assaults that wreak death and destruction upon innocent civilian populations.

To say that "violence never solves anything" is of course incorrect. As some of us have been pointing out for years, violence is a serviceable instrument of ruling-class control. That is why it is used so frequently and furiously. Violence is an effective resource of political power, one of the coercive instrumentalities used to convince others to submit to policies that are harmful to themselves but beneficial to the interests of global investors. US leaders often use violence or other forms of repressive coercion to destroy dissenting individuals, organizations, governments, and the living standards of whole societies, as done recently to Iraq and Yugoslavia. Of course, the quick and vicious success that violence brings can create problems of its own, one of these being terrorism, which is most likely to emerge when a suppressed democratic opposition mutates into a virulent religious strain.

Superpower applications of violence have successfully eradicated popular movements that attempt to benefit the general populace. US global policy is devoted to benefiting the few not the many. This global policy must be opposed not because it is a failure but because it has been so terribly successful in the service of the rich and powerful, at great cost to the American people and still greater cost to the peoples of many other lands.

Capitalism operates with utmost success in countries like Indonesia, El Salvador, and the Congo where the rate of accumulation is highest and poverty is deepest. The more desperately poor are the people, the harder will they work for less. So the Third World is capitalism at its best, at its freest, the place where it is least troubled by labor unions, high wages, work benefits, occupational safety regulations, consumer protections, environmental controls, costly social benefits, public sector services, business taxes, and other progressive taxes. For half a century, commentators have been talking about bringing the prosperity of the Western world to the Third World. What is overlooked is that the real goal has been the other way around: to bring the Third World to the Western world, rolling back the century of democratic gains won by working people in North America and Europe.

As US politico-economic elites become increasingly successful at expanding their global power and privileges, life on this planet becomes increasingly difficult. The human rights and life chances of millions of people throughout the world are increasingly under siege. The systemic terrorism of transnational exploitation takes a horrifying toll. Some 35,000 children die every day from hunger or poverty-related diseases. The number of people living in utter destitution without hope of relief is growing at a faster rate than the world's population. So poverty spreads as wealth accumulates.

Meanwhile, the planet's very ecology is put at risk. The quality of the air we breathe and water we drink is deteriorating; forests are being turned into wastelands; our farmlands are being depleted of topsoil by agribusiness; chemical toxins contaminate the entire food chain; species are being driven into extinction; and ozone depletion and global warming threaten to become irreversible in their cumulative effects. Yet those who control the productive powers of society insist that all is well, and continue to treat the earth's dwindling resources as an inexhaustible disposable commodity to be used at will for the maximization of private profits.

What is needed is a 180 degree shift away from unilateral global domination and toward equitable betterment and sustainable development among the peoples of the world. This means US leaders would have to stop acting like self-willed unaccountable rulers of the planet. They must stop supporting despots, and stop opposing those democratic movements and governments that challenge the socio-economic status quo. The struggle is between those who believe that the land, labor, capital, technology, markets, and natural resources of society should be used as expendable resources for transnational profit accumulation, and those who believe that such things should be used for the mutual benefit of the populace.

What we need is to move away from liberal complaints about how bad things are and toward a radical analysis that explains *why* they are so, away from treating every situation as a perfectly new and befuddling happening unrelated to broader politico-economic interests and class power structures. What we need is a global anti-imperialist movement that can challenge the dominant paradigm with an alternative one, that circumvents the monopoly ideological control of officialdom and corporate America.

We not only need such a movement, we already have one as manifested by the mass protests in Seattle, Quebec City, Washington, Philadelphia, Los Angeles, Prague, Sidney, Genoa, Perugia, and other places too numerous to mention. Against all odds, all monopoly propaganda, all deception and intimidation, against the most hopeless situations, we continue to struggle as we have in the past, sometimes even winning victories and making gains.

More people around the world are coming to see that their leaders are running the cruelest scam in history, and that the conditions we face are not the outgrowth of happenstance but the result of concerted and intentional rapacity, the creation of poverty by wealth, the creation of powerlessness by the powerful—a cycle we must yet someday reverse if we want our prosperity and liberties extended more equitably and securely, and if we want life on our planet to survive in a healthful form.

Those who believe in democracy must not be taken in by the reactionism that cloaks itself in patriotic hype. They must continue in their determination to educate, organize, and act. In any case, fighting against the current is always preferable to being swept away by it.

Notes to Chapter 1: Terrorism Meets Reactionism

1 *Wall Street Journal*, editorial, September 19, 2001.

2 See the discussion in chapter five.

3 John Pilger, "The Real Story behind America's War," *New Statesman*, December 17, 2001.

4 *New York Times*, December 13, 2001.

5 By the "US national security state" I mean the Executive Office of the White House, the National Security Council, National Security Administration, Central Intelligence Agency, Federal Bureau of Investigation, and other such units engaged in surveillance, suppression, covert action, and interventions abroad and at home. Also included are the monitoring committees set up by the NSC, such as the "54/12 Group," later known in the Nixon era as the "40 Committee," composed of top players from State, Defense, the CIA, the Joint Chiefs of Staff, the White House, and the NSC itself.

6 Quoted in Tim Wheeler, "Bush Plan Puts Profits before Air Security," *People's Weekly World*, November 10, 2001

7 See the discussion in chapter five.

8 These several examples are mentioned by Lewis Lapham, "Notebook: American Jihad," *Harper's*, January 2002.

9 USA PATRIOT is a dismal acronym for Uniting and Strengthening America by Providing Appropriate Tools Required to Intercept and Obstruct Terrorism.

10 For a good critique, see Nancy Chang, "The USA PATRIOT Act," *CovertAction Quarterly*, Winter 2001. For additional information on the USA PATRIOT Act, see the American Civil Liberties Union website: www.aclu.org.

11 Wheeler, "Bush Plan Puts Profits before Air Security."

12 For an overview, see Senator Byron Dorgan, "Global Shell Games: How the Corporations Operate Tax Free" <http://www.washingtonmonthly.com/features/2000/0007. dorgan.html>.

Notes to Chapter 2: The September 11 Obsession

13 For information on US terrorist interventions throughout the world and over the years, see my *Against Empire* (San Francisco: City Lights Books, 1995); my *Inventing Reality*, 2nd edition (New York: Bedford/St. Martin's, 1993); William Blum, *Rogue State* (Monroe, Maine: Common Courage, 2000); and Edward Herman, *The* Real *Terrorism Network* (Boston: South end Press, 1982).

14 Louis Freedberg, *San Francisco Chronicle*, December 30, 2001.

15 Report by Citizens for Tax Justice, cited in *Wall Street Journal*, October 17, 2001.

16 Armey quoted in Bill Moyers, "Which America Will We Be Now?" *Nation*, November 19, 2001.

17 Arthur Perlo, "Wall Street's Patriotism?" *People's Weekly World*, November 3, 2001. The *Times* quote is in Perlo's article.

18 Kathleen Pender, "Picking War Stocks is Hell," *San Francisco Chronicle*, December 20, 2001.

19 *Washington Post*, December 7, 2001.

20 *Washington Post*, October 21, 2001.

21 *Washington Post* op-ed, September 20, 2001.

22 Lori Wallach and Michelle Sforza, *World Trade Organization? Corporate Globalization and the Erosion of Democracy* (Washington, D.C.: Public Citizen, 1999); and *FTAA for Beginners* (Boston, Mass.: United for a Fair Economy, January 2001).

23 David Broder in the *Washington Post*, noted by Lewis Lapham, "Notebook: American Jihad," *Harper's*, January 2002.

Notes to Chapter 3: Why Did It Happen?

24 Mark Juergensmeyer, *Terror in the Mind of God* (Berkeley: University of California Press, 2000), 6.

25 Juergensmeyer, *Terror in the Mind of God*, 20-26.

26 Juergensmeyer, *Terror in the Mind of God*, 113.

27 *New York Times*, December 15, 2001.

28 See Arundhati Roy, "The Algebra of Infinite Justice," *Guardian* (London), September 29, 2001.

29 Madison Shockley, "Why Do They Hate Us? Let African Americans Count the Ways," *San Francisco Chronicle*, December 9, 2001.

30 Robert M. Bowman, "What Can We Do About Terrorism?" *North Coast Xpress*, Winter 2001.

31 The above data and quotation are from Christian Parenti and Christopher D. Cook, "Empire's Terrors," *San Francisco Bay Guardian*, September 19, 2001.

32 Parenti and Cook, "Empire's Terrors."

33 Parenti and Cook, "Empire's Terrors."

34 Parenti and Cook, "Empire's Terrors."

35 Joyce Chediac, "Turkey, the Secret El Salvador," *Workers World*, February 19, 1982; and Mehmet Demir, "Turkey: Repression Tightens Grip," *Guardian* (New York), September 12, 1984.

36 *New York Times*, December 15, 2001.

37 Arundhati Roy, "The Algebra of Infinite Justice," *Guardian* (London), September 29, 2001.

38 Zakaria's views are summarized well by Michael Massing, "Press Watch," *Nation*, November 5, 2001.

39 *New York Times*, September 14, 2001.

40 *Washington Post*, Sept 20, 2001.

41 In a recent talk, Noam Chomsky was accused of blaming America by someone in the audience. Pointing to the questioner and then to himself, Chomsky said most emphatically, "I blame you, I blame me, I blame all of us for letting this happen": Massachusetts Institute of Technology, Boston, Technology and Culture Forum, November 18, 2001, video distributed by Ralph Cole at JusticeVision, http://www.justicevision.org.

42 *Washington Post*, December 21, 2001.

43 *San Francisco Chronicle*, December 9, 2001.

44 *Wall Street Journal/NBC poll, released November 12, 2001.*

45 *Nation*, November 19, 2001.

46 Michael Gordon, "Pentagon Corners Output of Special Afghan Images," *New York Times*, October 19, 2001.

47 Roberto J. Gonzalez, "Ignorance Is Not Bliss," San Francisco Chronicle, January 2, 2002.

48 *Washington Post*, December 21, 2001.

Notes to Chapter 4: Afghanistan, the Untold Story

49 For example, as of November 2001, Noam Chomsky continued to condemn the "Russian [sic] invasion of Afghanistan" and assert that "opposing the Russian invasion was a good thing": See his talk at Massachusetts Institute of Technology, Boston, Technology and Culture Forum, November 18, 2001, video distributed by Ralph Cole at JusticeVision, http://www.justicevision.org.

50 John Ryan, "Afghanistan: A Forgotten Chapter," *Canadian Dimensions*, November/December 2001; Phillip Bonosky, *Afghanistan: Washington's Secret War*, 2nd edition (New York: International Publishers, 2001).

51 Taraki was not anti-Islam. He declared a commitment to Islam within a secular state, and even paid part of the costs for operating mosques; see William Blum *Killing Hope* (Monroe, Maine: Common Courage Press, 1995), 340.

52 Marilyn Bechtel, "Afghanistan: Some Overlooked History," *People's Weekly World*

53 *San Francisco Chronicle*, November 17, 2001.

54 Arundhati Roy, "The Algebra of Infinite Justice," *Guardian* (London), September 29, 2001.

55 Amnesty International report quoted in *San Francisco Chronicle*, November 17, 2001.

56 Roy, "The Algebra of Infinite Justice."

57 Roy, "The Algebra of Infinite Justice."
58 *Los Angeles Times*, August 2, 1993; and William Blum. *Rogue State* (Monroe, Maine: Common Courage Press, 2000), 35.
59 See Ahmed Rashid, *Taliban: Militant Islam, Oil and Fundamentalism in Central Asia* (New Haven: Yale University Press, 2000).
60 Patrick Healy, "Kandahar Residents Feel Betrayed," *Boston Globe*, December 19. 2001.
61 On the reactionary influence of the early Christians, see my *History as Mystery* (San Francisco: City Lights, 1999), chapters two and three.
62 Ted Rall, "It's About Oil," *San Francisco Chronicle*, November 2, 2001.
63 United Nations International Drug Control Program, "Afghanistan Annual Opium Poppy Survey 2001" http://www.undcp.org/pakistan/report_2001-10-16_1.pdf
64 *Washington Post*, December 26, 2001.
65 Herold's study is referred to in San Francisco Chronicle, January 2, 2001.
66 Lawrence McGuire, "Small News: Killing Other People's Children," *Counter Punch*, December 20, 2001.
67 Both the Amnesty International report of November 2001 and the RAWA report are summarized in Terrie Albano "Afghan civilians at Risk in Alliance Takeover," *People's Weekly World*, November 17, 2001.
68 George J. Church, "Operation Steppe Shield," *Time*, March 18, 1991.
69 Terrie Albano, "What's Lurking Behind the War in Afghanistan?" *People's Weekly World*, November 17, 2001.
70 See the revealing account by Kemp Tolley, *Cruise of the Lani Kai* (Annapolis, Md.: Naval Institute Press, 1973)
71 Quoted in Tolley, *Cruise of the Lani Kai*, 302.
72 Patrick Martin, "US Planned War in Afghanistan long before September 11," World Socialist Conference, November 20,

2001, <http://www.wsws.org/articles/2001/nov 2001/afgh-n20.shtml>

73 Ryan, "Afghanistan: A Forgotten Chapter."

74 Michael Parenti, *Against Empire* (San Francisco: City Lights, 1995), 122.

Notes to Chapter 5: Why US Leaders Intervene Everywhere

75 "Imperialism" is a term not normally applied by mainstream commentators and academics to anything that US leaders do. So perhaps it needs a definition: imperialism, as used here, is the process whereby the rulers of one country use economic and military power to expropriate the land, labor, markets, and natural resources of another country in order to attain ever greater capital accumulations on behalf of wealthy interests at home and abroad.

76 For evidence in support of this see Michael Parenti, *Against Empire* (San Francisco: City Lights, 1995); Michael Parenti, *Inventing Reality*, 2nd edition (New York: St. Martin's, 1993); William Blum, *Killing Hope: US Military and CIA Interventions since World War II* (New York: Black Rose Books, 1998); and the writings of James Petras, Morris Morely, Edward Herman, and various others. For Petras's latest treatment of imperialism and capitalism, see his "Neo Mercantilist Empire in Latin America: Bush, ALCA and Plan Colombia" (unpublished monograph, 2001).

77 See Ingo Muller, *Hitler's Justice* (Cambridge, Mass.: Harvard University Press, 1991), part 3, "The Aftermath"; and Jon Wiener, "Bringing Nazi Sympathizers to the US," *Nation*, March 6, 1989, 306-309. Nazi war criminals have been aided by Western intelligence agencies, business interests, the military, and even the Vatican. In October 1944, German paratroop commander Major Walter Reder, slaughtered 1,836

defenseless civilians in a village near Bologna, Italy as a reprisal against Italian partisan activities. He was released from prison in 1985, after Pope John Paul II, among others, made an appeal on his behalf—over the strenuous protests of families of the victims.

78 Herbert Lottman, *The Purge* (New York: William Morrow, 1986), 290.

79 Hugh Deane, "Korea, China and the United Sates: A Look Back," *Monthly Review*, Feb. 1995, 20 and 23.

80 Roy Palmer Domenico, *Italian Fascists on Trial, 1943-1948* (Chapel Hill: University of North Carolina Press, 1991), passim.

81 *La Repubblica*, April 9, 1995; *Corriere della Sera*, March 27 and 28, 1995, April 12, 1995, and May 29, 1995.

82 Peter Gowan, "The NATO Powers and the Balkan Tragedy," *New Left Review*, March-April 1999,103-104.

83 Network news reports, October 27 to November 4, 1983; *New York Times*, November 6 to 20, 1983; John Judis, "Grenadian Documents Do Not Show What Reagan Claims," and Daniel Lazare, "Reagan's Seven Big Lies about Grenada," both in *In These Times*, November 6, 1983.

84 See the discussion of Grenada in my *Inventing Reality: The Politics of News Media*, 2nd edition (New York: St. Martin's Press, 1993[now available through Wadsworth]), 148-151.

85 "A Tottering Structure of Lies," *Sojourner*, December 1983, 4-5; and Michael Massing, "Grenada Before and After," *Atlantic Monthly*, February 1984, 79-80.

86 See "Special Report," *Labor* Action (publication of the Labor Coalition on Central America, Washington, D.C.), July/August 1990; Clarence Lusane, "Aftermath of the US Invasion," *CovertAction Information Bulletin*, Spring 1991, 61-63.

87 Quoted in William Appleman Williams, "American Intervention in Russia: 1917-1920," in David Horowitz (ed.), *Containment and Revolution* (Boston: Beacon Press, 1967), 36, 38.

88 *New York Times*, February 3, 1953.

89 Quoted in Richard Barnet, "The Uses of Force," *New Yorker*, April 29, 1991, 90.

90 When the text of Clinton's speech was printed the next day in the *New York Times*, the sentence quoted above was omitted. Observers who heard the speech reported the disparity.

91 Sean Gervasi, "Germany, US and the Yugoslav Crisis," *CovertAction Quarterly*, winter 1992-93, 41-42. Michel Chossudovsky, "Dismantling Former Yugoslavia, Recoloniz-ing Bosnia," *CovertAction Quarterly*, Spring 1996; and Chossudovsky's "Banking on the Balkans," THIS, July-August 1999.

92 *Interim Agreement for Peace and Self-government in Kosovo* (the "Rambouillet Agreement"), February 23, 1999, reproduced in full in full in *The Kosovo Dossier*, 2nd ed.(London: Lord Byron Foundation for Balkan Studies, 1999).

93 Gregory Elich, "The CIA's Covert War," *CovertAction Quarterly*, April-June 2001, 35-36.

94 Elich, "The CIA's Covert War," 38-39.

95 *Financial Times*, April 11, 2001; and a communication to me from Barry Lituchy, editor of *Eastern European Review*.

96 Jonathan Marshall, Peter Dale Scott, and Jane Hunter, *The Iran-Contra Connection* (Boston: South End, 1988); *Report of the Congressional Committee Investigating the Iran-Contra Affair* (Washington, D.C.: Government Printing Office, 1987).

97 Christopher Hitchens, *The Trial of Henry Kissinger* (London & New York: Verso, 2001), 98-99.

98 Ralph Miliband, *The State in Capitalist Society* (New York: Basic Books, 1969), 84 (italics in the original).

99 Lawrence Korb, "Perfect Time to Cut Military Spending," *San Francisco Chronicle*, December 31, 2001.